Johann Sebastian Bach

THE MASTER AND HIS WORK

Da Capo Press Music Reprint Series

Johann Sebastian Bach

THE MASTER AND HIS WORK

By

WILIBALD GURLITT

Translated by

OLIVER C. RUPPRECHT

New Introduction by

KARL GEIRINGER

Da Capo Press • New York • 1986

Library of Congress Cataloging in Publication Data

Gurlitt Wilibald, 1889–1963.
  Johann Sebastian Bach.

  (Da Capo Press music reprint series)
  Translation of: Johann Sebastian Bach.
  Reprint. Originally published: St. Louis: Concordia Pub. House, 1957.
With new introd.
  Includes index.
  1. Bach, Johann Sebastian, 1685–1750. 2. Composers—Germany—
Biography. I. Title.
ML410.B1G972   1986   780'.92'4 [B]   84-17664
ISBN 0-306-76262-5

This Da Capo Press reprint edition of *Johann Sebastian Bach: The Master and His Work* is an unabridged republication of the edition published in St. Louis in 1957, here supplemented with a new introduction by Karl Geiringer. It is reprinted by arrangement with Bärenreiter-Verlag.

Published by Da Capo Press, Inc.
A Subsidiary of Plenum Publishing Corporation
233 Spring Street, New York, N.Y. 10013

INTRODUCTION

Wilibald Gurlitt (1889–1963) belonged to a family of
artists and scholars. His father was a well known architect and art historian, his cousin a composer of world-
wide fame. Wilibald himself was a music historian who
was active as Professor at the West German University
of Freiburg, near the Swiss border. In 1937 the Nazi
government removed him from his position to which
he could only return eight years later.

Gurlitt aimed at recreating earlier music in the
most authentic manner and established a Collegium
Musicum that excelled in the performance of music
of the past. In particular, compositions of the Baroque
period fascinated the scholar and he was instrumental
in having an organ built which in every detail followed
early Baroque precepts. Gurlitt served also for a time as
the editor of the famous Riemann *Musik-Lexikon* which
he greatly improved and enlarged. In addition, he
started work on a monumental dictionary of musical
terminology — a project that has been successfully continued after his death.

These variegated activities provided the solid basis for the present study on Johann Sebastian Bach's life and art. This little book vividly portrays not only the composer himself but also his forebears and the social, religious, and political conditions that helped to mold Sebastian's personality. Written with penetrating insight and deep love for its subject, the work provides an incisive picture of the man and artist Bach. There is hardly another book of this size which brings Johann Sebastian's personality closer to our own thinking and feeling.

KARL GEIRINGER
Santa Barbara, California
January, 1985

Johann Sebastian Bach

THE MASTER AND HIS WORK

By

WILIBALD GURLITT

Translated by

OLIVER C. RUPPRECHT

CONCORDIA PUBLISHING HOUSE
SAINT LOUIS, MISSOURI

PREFACE

THE American translation of Dr. Wilibald Gurlitt's *JOHANN SEBASTIAN BACH — Der Meister und sein Werk* * has been carefully checked by Dr. Gurlitt and by the editorial staff of the American publisher. Despite these precautionary measures possible errors in the translation may have remained unnoticed. I shall be grateful to have these reported to me.

Many of the quotations occurring in Dr. Gurlitt's book had already been translated in *The Bach Reader,* edited by Hans T. David and Arthur Mendel. For more than one reason it seemed best to use the translation there provided. I am grateful to W. W. Norton and Company, Inc., for permission to incorporate extensive selections from that volume in the present translation.

For the convenience of those who wish to use Dr. Gurlitt's book for study or reference, I have prepared an index and a table of contents, besides marking or arranging the material itself so that divisions will be readily recognizable. The bibliography, prepared by Dr. Gurlitt for this translation, is another feature of the American edition.

Churchgoers and lovers of church music owe a debt of gratitude to the Bärenreiter Verlag for permission granted to make Dr. Gurlitt's appraisal of Bach's person and work available in English. The consent given by the Bärenreiter Verlag is a notable contribution in promoting the practice of a musical church art that will direct men's minds and hearts to the glory of our Redeemer and that will enable children of God to approximate the spiritual stature of one of the most heroic men of faith — J. S. Bach.

OLIVER C. RUPPRECHT

* Published by Bärenreiter Verlag, Kassel and Basel, 1949. The translation is based on the third edition.

CONTENTS

I

FAMILY BACKGROUND

TRADITION, origin, and heritage constitute the foundation of all truly great artistic creativity. If anyone demands proof for this assertion it will be best to point him to the generation of Thuringian Bachs. There is no more convincing evidence than that which is provided by the family from which the genius of Johann Sebastian Bach sprang. In the history of that family we see the magnificent drama of the rise of a clan comparable to the growth of a mighty oak. Grounded firmly by means of deep and widespread roots, the tree grows to towering heights and ultimately unfolds its culminating glory in a crown symbolic of power and strength. The endowments and achievements of this remarkable family increase from generation to generation, reach a high point of great splendor and then decline.

A reference to the importance of tradition, origin, and heritage is particularly fitting in a discussion of the Bach family, since Johann Sebastian Bach himself clearly realized that his own genius was deeply rooted in the sturdy growth and development of his forebears. To be a Bach meant for him to have received an inheritance deserving the highest esteem. The inheritance was precious; it had constantly been added to by the fathers; and it urged its possessor onward to an ever greater and more glorious unfolding of its possibilities. Accordingly, art, for Bach, was synonymous with accepting this heritage and with appropriating it by means of study, experience, and practice. Thus his pride of artistry was at the same time pride of ancestry and of family. We ought to note carefully, however, that Bach's sense of pride stemmed from the feeling of having received a noble calling and a solemn obligation; moreover, that his pride was utterly removed from the individualistic, egotistical vaingloriousness found in many artists.

Bach viewed his own life as a repetition of the existence of his ancestors. For that reason mastery in his art appeared to him not so much as a gift but as an assignment and a demand; he felt that he was confronted by something in which he was to achieve proficiency, to acquire expertness, and which he was to put into action. "Occasionally he was asked what measures he had undertaken to reach so high a degree of skill in his art. He usually replied: 'I have had to be diligent. If anyone will be equally diligent, he will be able to accomplish just as much.' He did not make much of, even as he did not depend on, his superior native endowments." (Forkel.)

Was Bach, the master, really conscious of the importance of tradition, origin, and heritage? Was he aware of the influence of these three factors as

8

constituting a living, active force giving form to the development of his genius? Did he appreciate the benefits resulting from an exchange of influence between these three and artisanship, labor, and toil? To arrive at an answer, we need follow no circuitous route nor employ circumstantial evidence. He himself has provided black-on-white testimony in the genealogical record which he began and which his granddaughter, Anna Carolina Philippina, the daughter of Philipp Emanuel Bach, continued. It bears the title: "Origin of the Musical-Bachian Family." It begins with the following sentences concerning the primal ancestor, Veit Bach:

> Vitus Bach, a baker in Hungary, was forced to leave Hungary in the 16th century because of the Lutheran religion. Thereupon he sold as many of his goods as possible and came to Germany. Since he found that Thuringia offered adequate security for the practice of the Lutheran religion, he settled in Wechmar, near Gotha. Here he continued to ply his trade *(Profession)* as a baker. He derived his greatest delight and pleasure from a cithara (little lute). He was in the habit of taking the instrument along into the mill and of playing it while the mill was a-grinding. What a pretty noise the two must have made together! Nevertheless, the combination was helpful in this way that he learned to keep time. And this is, so to speak, what provided the beginning of music among his descendants.

These sentences in the family chronicle, describing the human and the artistic personality of Bach's primogenitor, give clear and unmistakable prominence to three fundamental forces. These three forces

9

are of decisive significance for the natural, personal, and historico-spiritual bequests received by the Bach family. The first of these is the *sphere of home life (Heimatwelt)* in the region of East Central Germany. The second is the *world of faith and religion (Glaubenswelt)* of the Evangelical Lutheran Church. The third — in complete harmony with the world of faith and of home — is the *sphere of professional activity (Berufswelt)* of the citizen-musician *(stadtbuergerlicher Spielmann)*.

HOME LIFE

The Bach family lived as a generation of farmers and artisans in the region of Meissen, Thuringia, and Saxony. This territory was the home of German mysticism and of the Reformation by Martin Luther. A picture of Sebastian Bach's father, the only picture that has been preserved, is of special interest in this connection. Looking through a window in the picture we can see the Wartburg in the background. The old castle recalls to our mind the era of the landgraves, of the war of the singers, of St. Elizabeth, and of Junker Jörg (Luther's pseudonym in the Wartburg). This historically important structure lends an air of authenticity to this region. In the center of this area, in Arnstadt, Erfurt, and Eisenach, the Bachs held their joyful family holidays according to the ancient tradition of joint musicianship and *quodlibet*-singing.

Veit Bach was a native of Wechmar, a little town on the highway from Gotha to Arnstadt, not far from the home of Meister Eckhart. Wechmar was named after St. Vitus, the patron saint of the church and of the vicinity of Wechmar. As a member of a company of millers, Veit Bach had joined the trek of Central Germans who journeyed eastward. He had plied his trade in Hungary but was forced to flee because of his confessional loyalty to the Lutheran faith. The Counter Reformation of Rudolf II had been cruel and relentless. After Veit had sold his business in Hungary, he returned to his ancient home in Thuringia. He settled in Wechmar and, having taken a wife, lived near the lower mill, which has thus become the cradle of the musical branch of the Bach family.

The currents of political and cultural interrelationships between the regions of East Germany and the Slavic area, even into the vicinity of Pressburg and Siebenbürgen, may be traced back beyond the time of St. Elizabeth. Intercourse between Central Germany and the cities and settlements of Upper Hungary was provided chiefly through the cloisters but also by the artisan-citizens of the day. Moreover, the new Wittenberg movement found support at the royal court of Hungary. Here German life and Reformation faith stood in conflict with Slavic life and the movement of the Counter Reformation.

In the world of music the art of minor musicians in Central Germany (gathered about Georg Rhau in Wittenberg and Johannes Walter in Torgau) was brought eastward to Hungary at an early date and was carefully cultivated there. Among the leading German composers of the day Heinrich Finck lived at the Polish court and Thomas Stoltzer at the court of Hungary. On the other hand, the newly won Slavic territory exerted an influence on the instru-

11

mental music found in Central Germany. When Veit Bach, the miller, played on his lute, he may still have heard echoes of Hungarian music and may have remembered the intriguing skill of Valentin Bakfark, a skillful lutenist.

FAITH AND PIETY

In addition to the world of home life, the family chronicle emphasizes the *world of Lutheran belief* as a fundamental force in the existence of the Bach clan. There is an important contrast here between the later and earlier Bachs. Philipp Emanuel does not find it within himself to do more than merely to report the religious spirit animating the elder Bachs. He tells us that his ancestors "were in the habit of beginning all things with religion." By way of contrast to this detached and objective report, the deep-seated piety of Veit Bach, because it was original, personal, and militant, appears before us in a definite and clearly marked outline.

The form assumed by this religious spirit ignored neither the organized church nor her confessional writings. The piety of the early Bachs was that of the Lutheran Church in the age of orthodoxy. It was a piety bound strictly to confessional declarations. This kind of piety bore precious fruit in the life of Veit Bach. It brought forth faithfulness to the evangelical faith as proclaimed in the Reformation message of Luther. It produced a heroic spirit earnestly struggling for the truth and for purity in the confessional writings. It enabled him to stand firmly in the unshakable confidence of his faith. It moved

12

him to assume responsibility for his faith courageously and gladly, even in the midst of trouble and persecution.

Thus the founder of the musical-Bachian family comes before us as a resolute man of faith. He proclaims the Word of God in Lutheranism's warring church, the church of that religious movement from which German music and music culture obtained so many of its leaders and guides. When this powerful spiritual reality has lost its validity, has ceased to support and unite, we lose what these men possessed: their simple, direct understanding of art. It has been replaced by a broken, fragmentary view, dependent on a socio-historical development.

At the same time the literature and performance of music that gave Veit Bach "the greatest pleasure" seems to have consisted not so much in the spiritual and secular poetizing and singing ability of his day as in the playing of instruments. In regard to his playing of the lute the family chronicle expressly states that its beat, i. e., its rhythm (not the melody), was learned from the uniform sound of the mill wheels and the deep, peaceful currents of the millstream. In the compulsory uniformity of movement provided by the playing of his water mill, the primal Bach seems to have found the characteristic movement of that instrumental and rhythmically strong performance which, "so to speak, provided the beginning of music among his descendants." We are reminded here of the fundamentally rhythmic form of Sebastian Bach's instrumental music. We think of its constantly "ongoing" basses and their comprehensive ostinato. We are reminded, too, of the uninterrupted and pauseless motion of its "running basses" (basso continuo) and its rhythmic reflection in the music of all voices in polyphonic settings.

PROFESSIONAL ACTIVITY

Thus Veit Bach was a *Spielmann,* a musician in the garb of a miller. By means of his activity as a performer of music he simultaneously laid the foundation for the vocational world of the Bach family of musicians. All of his descendants, in a direct line to the father of Sebastian, were *Spielleute (musici instrumentales).* They plied their guildlike trade as town pipers and professional violinists, as musicians employed by town councils and at royal courts.

We have a good illustration in Veit's son, Johannes Bach, the great-grandfather of Sebastian. The family chronicle says: "At first he entered the profession of bakers. But because he had a strong inclination toward music, the town piper in Gotha took him into apprenticeship. At that time the old Castle Grimmenstein was still standing. According to the custom of the day, Johannes' superior and teacher lived in the castle tower. Even after Johannes had served the full term of apprenticeship, he remained for a while with his teacher." After the death of his father, Johannes Bach had married in Wechmar. In the years that followed "he was frequently sent to Gotha, Arnstadt, Erfurt, Eisenach, Smalcald, and Suhl, having received recommendations to help the town musicians in those municipalities."

In the same manner, Sebastian's grandfather and father, Christoph and Johann Ambrosius Bach, were

14

members of music guilds. Concerning Christoph Bach the family chronicle submits the following report: "He, too, learned instrumental music. At first he was employed at the Court of Weimar, where his rank entitled him to service from the Duke's servants. Later he found employment in a company of town musicians, first in Erfurt and then in Arnstadt." Moreover, it was a musician — Sebastian Nagel, town piper of Gotha — who at the occasion of Sebastian's baptism in the Church of St. George in Eisenach, held his godchild over the baptismal font. Sebastian's older brother Johann Jakob, too, learned the musicians' trade from his father, whom he succeeded in the office of town trumpeter in Eisenach.

We may well regard Hans Bach (1555—1615) as a characteristic type of these early Bachian musicians. He was probably a brother of Veit. Combining the role of musician and artisan in one person, he, too, journeyed from Wechmar into strange territory, urged onward by Bachian wanderlust. Wherever he went, he was known and loved for his humorous inspiration and his ability to make people laugh. He seems to have inherited some of the spirit of the traveling musicians and clownish performers of earlier days. When he arrived at the Court of Württemberg, he was already graying at the temples. The court musicians were under the direction of Leonhard Lechner and Basilius Froberger, the father of the great composer of piano music. These men raised music at the Württemberg court to a highly flourishing state. Hans Bach was in the service of the youthful widow, Countess Ursula. He died on her estate in Nürtlingen in the Neckar Valley.

15

Two pictures of Hans Bach have been preserved by Philipp Emanuel Bach in his collection of family pictures. The one presents him as musician and court jester, equipped with violin and decorated with the court fool's cap and bells. The picture is accompanied by the following verse:

> Here you behold the fiddler Hans Bach.
> Whenever he plays, you have to laugh.
> He plays in a manner entirely his own,
> And his beard is most handsome, for which
> he is known.

On the other picture he looks somewhat surly. Dressed in courtly garb, he carries the equipment of journeying musicians. In the left hand he carries an artistic descant violin. His right hand holds a well-filled drinking mug. He is surrounded by carpenter's tools and a harlequin's (wooden) sword with a bell. The legend provides the following information: "Hans Bach, morio celebris et facetus, fidicen rediculus, homo laboriosus, simplex et pius" — well-known and whimsical mischiefmaker, jocose fiddler, a diligent, simple, and pious man. These words describe not only Hans Bach but the whole tribe of Bach musicians: they were animated by a spirit which we correctly designate as industrious, plain, and God-fearing.

In 1635 the Bach homestead was transferred from Wechmar, the cradle of the family of Bach musicians, to *Erfurt*. The oldest of the Bach musicians entered Erfurt in that year. A brother of the great Heinrich Schütz had become syndic of the city in the same year; subsequently he became a professor at the University of Erfurt, and was later

16

made rector of the same institution. In Michael Altenburg, whose last service was rendered as pastor of the Andreaskirche, Erfurt possessed a notable musician. He had been a friend of Michael Praetorius. In Erfurt the grandfather of Sebastian, as well as his brother, was active, the former as *Ratsspielmann* (employed by the city council), the latter as organist in the Predigerkirche. Here Sebastian's father was born in 1645; he was baptized here, together with his twin brother Johann Christoph, in the Kaufmannskirche. At the age of twenty-two years he had obtained a position in the service of the Erfurt *Ratsspielmann*. A year later he found a life companion in the daughter of a family of artisans. Long established in Erfurt, they were originally well to do, but in the course of time lost their wealth. The girl, Elisabeth Lämmerhirt, was to become the mother of Sebastian.

Here in Erfurt Sebastian's sister was married. Here scholars discovered the only known picture of the youthful Sebastian, a portrait which is now a prized possession of the Erfurt Museum. Here Johann Christoph, Sebastian's brother, studied under Johann Pachelbel, the highly renowned organist of the Predigerkirche. For his predecessor Johann Bach, a brother of Christoph, the church had received a new organ, built by the leading organ builder of that day in Central Germany, Ludwig Compenius.

In Erfurt, this ancient Bach city, musicians had formed their own vocational order ever since the fifteenth century. In that period they had advanced to the position of *Kunstpfeifer* and had become "respectable." They had separated themselves from the beer fiddlers and the singers of cheap and banal songs. As town musicians they were joined in a "Company of Council Musicians" (*Rats-Musikanten-Compagnie*) consisting of four to six men, depending on the four- or six-voice structure of their canzoni, sonatas, suites, and dances. The *Direktor* was their chief. In this company the members of the Bach clan so greatly outnumbered all other performers that for a long time afterward musicians in Erfurt were called "the Bachs." This practice persisted even into later years, when the citizenry of Erfurt no longer included a single person by the name of Bach.

There is a living remnant of medieval communal life in this intimate association of the Erfurt musicians. Musicians, town musicians, and organists lived close together in the Erfurt musicians' quarter at the *Junkersand*. The grandparents, parents, and nearest relatives of Sebastian Bach lived in dwellings which were erected here, and some of those residences are still standing. Thus these men, musicians of the rank and caliber of Johann Pachelbel, Heinrich Buttstädt, and Johann Gottfried Walther, grew up in closest intimacy, the house of one adjoining the home of the other.

The town pipers *(Stadtpfeifer)* performed the duties of their life's calling in the spirit of the Middle Ages; that is to say, they made no great distinction between artist and artisan. This basic principle of their existence manifested itself in a characteristic and individual manner of living. The preservation of rank and of other vocational classifications among the musicians of Bach's own time is mirrored plainly in the fightings and disputes about

18.

inherited rights and privileges, about social custom, about honor and living standards. The struggle raged continually between cantors and organists, organists and town pipers, town pipers and beer fiddlers. Innumerable accounts of these conflicts are found in the music history of every German city and community of Bach's time as well as in the novels of that day. This distinction in rank was carried farther, from the town musicians' and organists' life as citizens into the academic world of cantors in church and school. It extended even into the world of the performer of chamber music, whose life was spent at court.

Because of their common university background, cantors (from the Latin *canere,* to sing) were usually classified together with ministers and schoolmasters. This fact is evident from the frequency with which the three were grouped together. Cantors and organists, however, were grouped together only in exceptional instances. An old proverb said: "Organisten — schlechte Christen" ["Organists are poor Christians"]. By way of contrast, we find that organists and town musicians *(Stadtpfeifer)* were closely associated in their daily living, either as friends, baptismal sponsors, or relatives. A prominent Leipzig citizen applied for the position of cantor in St. Thomas' Church. He was not only a town musician, but a composer. Yet his application was rejected, "because he had been a town musician here."

Even the music of these various vocational orders reflected this difference in the degree of rank. Each group had assigned to it its own style, based

19

on rhythmic considerations. The order of cantors received the *ecclesiastische* style; the order of organists, the *hyporchematische;* the order of town musicians, the *melismatische.* Long note values were regarded as a device by means of which one might recognize and identify the art of cantors. Only after the liberalistic tendencies of the Age of Enlightenment began to assert themselves, do we find that "artists" and "musicians" adopted a standard of living which was self-sufficient, altogether independent of the vocational activity within a certain branch of the world of art. Only then had the life of musicians become freed from considerations of nobility or citizenship.

The distinctions of rank in the world of music are still maintained by Johann Mattheson in his work: *Vollkommener Kapellmeister* (1739). He has high praise for the courtly world of the *Kapellmeister (capellae magister),* whom he calls "a learned officer of court and a composer of the highest rank." He bestows a similar encomium on the academic world of the *cantor,* whom he terms "a musically highly trained servant in church and school." Organists and musicians are compared unfavorably with these two groups. The organist, who lives in a world of ordinary citizens, is "a skillful servant of the church and a very able performer on the clavier." The *musician* and conventional performer is one whose chief virtue is cleverness: "that which has been placed before him he sings in a striking manner and plays very easily." The implication is that his performance achieves no lasting effect. Mattheson adds the humorous comment: "Whoever cannot at once obtain

20

the dignity of a *Kapellmeister,* either by force or by begging, usually permits himself to be reviled *(schelten)* by the title of *Musikdirektor.* Even such a designation is better than that of cantor or organist. In fact, many a person does not want to be called *Kapellmeister,* but composer of chamber music or of court compositions. Yet these expressions are poor, makeshift, and un-German."

Musicians of a lower order were joined, conceptually, with organists and with performers on a clavier by the manual or digital dexterity *(Fingerfertigkeit)* found among all of them. True enough, this basic similarity in their use of instruments had more to do with the work of an artisan than with the activity of an artist. But the moral implication of the proverb is clear: "To blow is not to play the flute; you must move the fingers." *(Blasen ist nicht flöten, ihr müsst die Finger bewegen.)* For the same reason the artistic distance from town piper to organist was not very great. The organ, as a richly sensuous *Pfeifen-Klavier,* incorporated within itself the professions of two artist-artisan groups: those who performed on wind instruments and those who performed on a keyboard (*clavis* = key; therefore the term *clavier*).

It is a characteristic trait in German musicians of former times to have a decided preference for proficiency in both fields; to be skilled performers of wind instruments and of keyboard instruments. In many a family the same person achieved this twofold proficiency. The fact that Sebastian Bach, in his position as *Thomaskantor,* was at the same time the supervisor of the Leipzig town pipers

21

and professional violinists and of their renowned director, Gottfried Reiche, was not due to his position as cantor but as "Director of Music" *(director musices)*. The latter office was the ecclesiastical counterpart of the office of a *Kapellmeister* at a royal court. Even this office was only semisecular in character. As late as 1700 there is no sharp distinction in the character of the music presented at a royal court, whether in the royal chambers, at the festive board, in the theater, or in the court church. The music is not classified as worldly or spiritual. Both forms, or elements, of music belong in the comprehensive and widely inclusive domain of church music, since all of them, at least in the more extended sense of the term, are forms of art placed into the service of God.

In Erfurt, too, as in other cities, the calling of the town player *(Spielmannsberuf)*, or performer, was a means of livelihood reserved for artists, who formed a kind of guild. Only a director installed by the government was authorized to keep apprentices and journeymen in his service. An apprentice served for five years. Having been declared free, he obtained a letter of recommendation and set out on an adventurous journey to find another master, one of his own choosing. He remained with him as an associate for three or five additional years, "in the service of art." Only at this stage was he permitted to apply for the position and rank of a master in a post that might happen to be available. To obtain it, he was compelled to give a trial performance under the surveillance of two masters and an associate. In addition to their regional grouping, the players and performers *(Spielleute)* of Central Germany had, since 1653, been gathered in an association enjoying imperial privileges. It bore the name *Instrumental-Musikalisches Collegium in dem Ober- und Nieder-Sächsischen Kreis.*

These players had only recently renounced an activity originally associated with the musical services rendered by their group. Formerly they had rendered the service of the *Hausmann,* as watchmen and in towers. Although eventually discharged, the *Hausmann* continued to exert an influence on the civic life of the town piper. His duties play a prominent role in the fictional novels and romances of that day. Even the great-grandfather of Sebastian had learned this trade from his master in the tower of the castle of Gotha.

After the town player had descended from the tower and had become a "citizen-musician" *(Bürger-Musikant),* he matured and reached a station of considerably greater significance. He became chiefly responsible for the preservation and promotion of the town's musical interests. Appointed by the town council, he received fees and other perquisites. The cost of his residence was paid in part. He received a uniform which bore the heraldic insignia of the town. Some of his pay was given in the form of products of the field. Other favors included gifts at New Year's Day and other festivals, musical instruments, and the privilege of counsel. Above all, however, he insisted that no one but he and his associates were permitted to serve in this particular capacity at civic festivals staged within the city limits, at weddings, baptisms, and similar occasions of fellowship

23

and banqueting. He was one of the most familiar figures in the daily life of the city. The services he was obliged to render were numerous and manifold. He provided music on the *Pfeiferstuhl* in council chambers, at the occasion of receptions, council elections, and other civic festivals. He supervised the nonlicensed players and wandering musicians who happened to be in the town. He had other duties: early in the morning, at noon, and in the evening of every day he ascended the tower of a church, castle, city hall, or city gate, to sound forth *(abblasen)* the hour of the day. From these same towers he was to welcome *(anblasen)* strangers and guests who approached the city. Here also he rang the tax bells on terminal days. In the evening he rang the fire bell from this spot, to indicate the time when the person in charge of a household was to cover fires (curfew) and lights.

Although the town piper took part in all folk festivals, guild gatherings, and family celebrations, the heavier musical demands made on him had to do with his assistance in the performance of church music. Before and after the sermon, especially on Sundays and feast days, he provided music in the churches of the city, supporting the work of choir and organ *(zu Chore blasen, in die Orgel musizieren)*. While rendering this service he came into contact with the cantor and the organist and their superior art.

His store of musical instruments consisted chiefly (as his name indicated) of wind instruments *(blasende)*, in addition to those that were to be played with a bow *(streichende)*. His rating as a musician

24

rose, however, in direct proportion to the number of instruments he could play. His musical equipment included the ability to play the instruments in the trombone and cornet families, oboes, bassoons, and other double-reed instruments, recorders, traverse flutes, trumpets, tympani, fifes, drums, violas da gamba, violas da braccio, and violins.

As early as the days of Sebastian Bach's father the professional trumpeters in the town trumpeters' orchestra were ranked with the professional violinists. The latter group had abandoned the gamba structure of their instrument and had adopted the conventional violin form. They called it a viola and a (Polish) violin. Of these, they preferred the descant type of violin; already Hans Bach, the musician, had been pictured with this instrument. Only the "disreputable" instruments of wandering and strolling musicians were excluded from the professional activity of the town musicians: *Dudelsack, Drehleier, Sackpfeife,* and *Triangel.*

By joining the instruments into "choirs," it was possible to present the four- and six-part selections of the town musicians in a variety of settings, the choice depending largely on the occasion and the location. At times the music is arranged for instruments that are closely related; at other times the setting is based on a heterogeneous grouping of wind and string instruments. In general, the influence of the practice continues prominently even in Sebastian Bach's instrumental and orchestral works. The notion that an instrumental musician might restrict his art to proficiency in regard to only a single instrument is an achievement of the large instrumental ensembles of the courts.

Although the conventional player *(Spielmann)* at one time performed his music from memory, even when appearing in ensemble, the town musician, on the other hand, usually "had a book in front of his nose." His repertoire consisted of the indigenous music flourishing in Germany about 1650. It ranged from the simple forms of spiritual and secular songs and dances to higher art forms. Beginning here with skillful *Intraden, Pavanen, Kanzonen, Ricercare,* and *Fantasien,* as preserved in the collections of "Tower- and Trumpet-Music" *(Turm- und blasende Musiken)* gathered by the Leipzig town trumpeters Joh. Christoph Petzold and Gottfried Reiche, these selections extend to the great sonatas, suites, and instrumental works of free and elaborate design, written by composers of Central Germany in the days of Matthias Weckmann and Johann Rosenmüller. The introductory and intermediary instrumental compositions in the cantatas, the orchestral suites, and the Brandenburg Concerti of Sebastian Bach belong in this line of musical invention.

As late as 1700 the professional activity of the town trumpeters, even in its simplest forms, was so highly regarded in the world of music that Johann Kuhnau, Bach's predecessor in Leipzig, could compare it with the music of heaven. In his *Musikalischer Quaksalber* (1700) he says: "When our town pipers sound forth from the tower, possibly at the occasion of a festival, and with loud trombones proclaim a spiritual song, all of us are deeply and immeasurably moved. We imagine that we hear the angels singing." [1]

All in all, the existence, the services, and the artistry of these town trumpeters were inextricably woven into the political, religio-ecclesiastical, social, and artistic life of the town and its citizens. In the morning these musicians roused the people from their slumber. In the evening they provided a suitable song. Thus they were a part of each day's course and of every passing year. Here, in this intimate penetration of all the circumstances and conditions of daily life, but also in the active and living use of the services of these men and of their skill, lies the deep and strong root which bound these town trumpeter-ancestors of Sebastian Bach and their art to a communal society, to the national life, and to the very landscape of the region which was their home.

Emanating from this world of town musicians, the young Johann Sebastian Bach rose above it, passing beyond the rank of organists into the realm of *Konzert- und Kapellmeister* in the royal courts. In 1671 his father had removed to Eisenach, where he sought to become the successor of the town piper. He gave a trial performance in the Georgenkirche and was promptly appointed by the town council. Located in the market place, the Georgenkirche was the principal church in Eisenach. The high tradition of church music which prevailed in this church

---

[1] This is a reference to the trombones of those days. The narrowness of their design in distinction from present-day trombones, gave them a bright, penetrating tone.

is indicated by a *Kantorenbuch* which has been preserved. It contains works by the best composers of Germany and the Netherlands in the time of the Reformation. Johann Christoph Bach, the cousin of Sebastian's father, was active in this church. The family chronicle calls him "the great and expressive composer." He wrote motets, cantatas, chorale preludes for organ, and variations for clavier. The works that have been preserved compare favorably with the works of his contemporaries Dietrich Buxtehude and Philipp Krieger. We need mention only the corlorful variations composed by Johann Christoph and based on an aria which had been written by his superior at the Eisenach court, *Kapellmeister* Eberlin (*Aria Eberliniana*, 1690). Or we might refer to the vividly declaimed Alto-Arioso (Lamento): "Ach, dasz ich Wassers genug hätte," which is written in the best tradition of the "speaking" style [see p. 89] found in the compositions of Heinrich Schütz. But this tendency toward the picturesque, joined with a talent for vivid portrayal, is, after all, a part of the artistic legacy of the Bach family.

In 1662 Eisenach was made the capital of the newly independent duchy, Sachsen-Eisenach. This political change brought with it certain important cultural developments. Formerly, a civic group had fostered the musical activities of the town pipers; a church group had been responsible for the training of the school choir and the *Kurrende* of the Latin school. This twofold program had represented the sum and substance of the town's musical efforts. To this there were now added the endeavors of a group at the royal court. The chamber music group at the

28

court attracted important musicians. Its membership included the father of Sebastian Bach. Pachelbel was assigned to it before he went to the Predigerkirche in Erfurt, from where he later went to Stuttgart, Gotha, and Nürnberg, the seat of his paternal ancestors.

As a pupil of Kaspar Kerll, organist at the court of Vienna, Pachelbel had become thoroughly familiar with the bel canto of the Italian violinists and organists. Known at the Eisenach court as a "perfect and rare virtuoso," Pachelbel increased in stature and became the leader, after Samuel Scheidt, of the music of performance in Central Germany. Not content to be the inheritor of a great tradition, Pachelbel enlivened and enriched it with his sonatas and suites written in several parts. He also contributed organ music which led in the direction of greater emotional content and a songlike, cantabile style. In Eisenach he gained the friendship of Sebastian's father and stood godfather to his second daughter, who, however, died at an early age. In Erfurt, Pachelbel became the teacher of Sebastian's father's eldest son, Johann Christoph, who since 1690 had been organist of the Michaeliskirche in nearby Ohrdruf.

In the fall of 1694 Johann Christoph Bach married the daughter of one of the members of the town council. Tradition has it that at the wedding of this same Johann Christoph Bach and the councilman's daughter in Ohrdruf, Johann Pachelbel, Ambrosius Bach, and the cousin of the latter, the town piper Hoffmann, "joined in a performance on the violin." It is possible that on this occasion the trio performed Pachelbel's three-part canon variations on a ground bass (basso ostinato), a composition which ends with a canzone-gigue for three violins and figured bass *(Generalbass)*. Truly, an instance in which the skill of town pipers reached a high degree of art!

These fourteen variations, whose structure reveals the most rigorous severity, can be discussed here only in their most essential features. We might, for example, call attention to the twofold manner in which the solo voice is bound to the genuinely three-voiced canon and to the ground bass. Or we might point to the gentle, songlike character of the ostinato itself, with its traditional motif of descending fourths. Again, we might observe the exemplary technique of these well-nigh perfect variations, as they move onward in a uniform kind of progress; the secret of their excellence lies in an apparently prosaic means — perfect mathematical and mechanical control, intensified in successive variations and derived almost as if by improvisation from the technical powers inherent in violin music. Or we might notice the rising intensity resulting from the joint activity of various voices suspended over an unalterably uniform bass whose theme is repeated thirty times. We might give attention also to the manner in which the increase in movement is accompanied by a corresponding growth in the richness and fullness of sensuous sound. Last but not least, we might admire the adornment beautifying the stark barrenness of the basic structure: the beauty is given by the songlike character prevailing throughout, and this continuing lyric flow and melodiousness, in turn, invests the entire work with the mighty power of strong and suggestive symbolism.

Here, then, is pure "music of performance," in the deepest and truest sense of the term. True enough, it is human work and human activity; yet it is not carried on for its own sake. Even as it derives its life from a faith focused on the Creation, so this music itself is a type and symbol of God's own order in Creation. It is art of the kind described by Andreas Werckmeister (1691) in the words: "Although music has its own external being and form, it is a beautiful reminder of the spiritual, heavenly Being and gives us occasion to think of that Being . . . even as music in general has this distinguishing characteristic that it is a mirror of the divine order and provides us with a foretaste of the heavenly harmony."

II

THE YOUNG MUSICIAN

CHILDHOOD AND YOUTH

ON March 21, 1685, the youngest child was born in the family of the Eisenach town trumpeter, Johann Ambrosius Bach, and his wife Elizabeth. Two days later the child was baptized in the Georgenkirche. He was named *Johann Sebastian Bach*. He received his first name from his father and his second name from his sponsor, Sebastian Nagel. This house on the Frauenplan, in which Bach was born, was home for a relatively large company of people. Not only Bach's parents, as well as several sisters and brothers (five in all), but also his father's apprentices and associates lived here.

Already as a boy of tenderest age young Sebastian drew inspiration and instruction from the age-old, uninterrupted tradition of the town musicians, a tradition firmly established in this area. His first teacher was his father. He learned the earliest rudiments of his father's profession and practiced them in the performance of violin music. "In his youth he played the violin in a manner noted for purity and penetration of tone. He continued to play the violin even in later years. By his mastery of the instrument he maintained control of the orchestra and achieved better order than would have been possible by means of a keyboard instrument." This is Philipp Emanuel's verdict concerning his father.

When Sebastian was nine years old, his mother died. His father, who had remarried shortly after the death of his first wife, followed her and was buried on February 24, 1695. When in later years we find Sebastian intimately acquainted with the figure of death, we must remember that this familiarity dates back to his life as a child, orphaned as he was in early boyhood. But of his own children, too, he carried eleven to the grave.

Sebastian's oldest brother had made a vocational transfer which removed him from their father's ancient profession. He left the town pipers and became an organist. The other two brothers continued to function as town pipers. Young Sebastian experienced a significant and fateful turn of events, therefore, when the Eisenach household was broken up and he was placed in the care of his oldest brother in Ohrdruf. His journey involved more than moving from one town to another. It brought about a vocational transition from *Spielmann* to organist.

Sebastian learned rapidly. His joy in instrumental practice was akin to a child's delight in games and in play. He was animated, in addition, by a burning desire and eagerness for learning. His studiousness quickly enabled him to master the keyboard art in which he had been instructed by his brother, the pupil of Pachelbel. As a result, he went beyond the instructional materials given him by his brother in Ohrdruf. He chose his own materials for study and practice. By playing and copying the works of contemporary masters of organ and Klavier, he made these masterpieces his own. At the same time he was on the lookout for a master teacher in the art of composition.

This early stage of learning, practicing, and acquiring is dependably described in the necrology of Sebastian Bach composed by Ph. Emanuel Bach and Sebastian's pupil Agricola and later enlarged by Mizler. The first act of young Sebastian to be recorded by a historian appears in the following account: "Within a short time he had completely learned *(völlig in die Faust gebracht)* all the pieces which his brother had voluntarily assigned to him for study. His brother, however, had another book, filled with keyboard compositions by the most famous masters of that day: Froberger, Kerll, Pachelbel. Despite all the pleas of Sebastian, his brother denied his requests, for reasons which we can only imagine. But Sebastian's earnest zeal, and his desire to make better progress in his chosen profession, prompted him to engage in the following innocent bit of deception. The book lay in a locked cabinet; access, however, could be obtained through the doors, which were without glass but were fitted with bars. At night, when everyone had gone to bed, he would take the book out of the cabinet. The withdrawal was possible because his small hands could pass

34

between the bars. Moreover, the book, bound only in paper, could be rolled up while still in the cabinet. Having removed the book he copied it by moonlight, since he could not even obtain a light for himself. After six months this musical prize was safely in his hands. Working secretly, he eagerly endeavored to make this music his own and to utilize it in his professional development. To his great sorrow, his brother discovered his deed and cruelly took from him the manuscript he had so laboriously copied."

The Ohrdruf Latin School was conducted according to the Gotha *Schulmethodus* of 1642. The broad and liberal sympathies of educational leaders like Ratke and Comenius permeated the school. Their attitude helped to bring about a greater appreciation of practical subjects. Young Sebastian attended this school. When Sebastian reached Prima, the *Schulkantor* Herda recommended Bach and Erdmann, his two most competent students, for acceptance without charge into the *Mettenchor* of the convent school of the Michaeliskirche in Lüneburg. Acceptance on this basis was limited to pupils "who are the children of poor people and possess good treble voices." Bach met both requirements. In later years Philipp Emanuel remembered to praise his father on this account, saying: "He had a good voice; it was pleasing and penetrating, and carried well."

Assured that he possessed a voice excellently adapted for singing, Bach went to Lüneburg with his schoolmate Erdmann. There he served as *Diskantist* (treble singer) of the *Kantorei* (class of choristers) of the Michaeliskirche. Thus he was enabled to extend and to deepen his knowledge of the art of motet- and cantata-writing as found in contemporary and older compositions. In Lüneburg it was Sebastian's privilege to meet the aged organist of the Nikolaikirche, Johann Jakob Loewe, whose father had been a resident of Eisenach; Loewe himself had received personal instruction and guidance from Heinrich Schütz. He met another fellow townsman: Georg Böhm, born in Hohenkirchen, near Ohrdruf. Böhm, organist at the Johanniskirche, had been a pupil of old Adam Reinken in Hamburg. Through Böhm Bach became acquainted with the great tradition of organ building and organ playing in vogue in Hamburg, Bremen, Lübeck, and other towns of the old Hanseatic League.

After his voice had changed, Bach followed the custom of his forefathers and undertook journeys to organists of an established reputation. Seeking out men of the highest rank, whom he planned to serve as an *Altgeselle,* he hoped to learn about the most recent developments and methods in the world of musical art. It was for this reason, for example, that he journeyed to Hamburg. Here he met Vincenz Lübeck, organist at the Nikolaikirche, and Adam Reinken, organist at the Katharinenkirche; here he also became acquainted with the early beginnings of German opera. On several occasions he journeyed to Celle. He was particularly attracted by the musicians maintained by the ducal court (the duchess was a French noblewoman subscribing to the Huguenot confession). He found great delight in hearing the French violinists, organists, and performers on the clavecin (harpsichord).

The Youthful Performer

When Bach was seventeen years old, the period of his apprenticeship ended, and he entered upon his professional career. Once again, instrumental work loomed most prominently; it was his skilled, virtuoso performance on instruments that marked the beginning of his activity as a master musician. Forkel gives the following description of Bach's mastery of keyboard instruments: "He played with so little movement of his fingers, and this movement, too, was so light, that one could hardly notice it. Only the first joints of the fingers moved; even in the most difficult passages his hand retained its rounded form. His fingers hardly left the keys; when he did raise them a little, it was hardly more than is needed in the execution of a trill. When the one finger had work to do, the other remained undisturbed in its position. The remaining parts of his body were drawn into activity to an ever lesser degree."

Such careful use of the keyboard is indicative not only of Bach's style of performance but also of the "instrumental" character of the keyboard instruments of his day — the clavichord, the clavicembalo (Kielflügel), and the organ. Bach's predilection for mechanical production of tone and for the sound of wind instruments caused him to assign a central position to the organ as "queen of instruments." The age in which he lived shared his view.

Bach's unprecedented proficiency in two-manual work and in pedal playing, as well as in organ registration, proved to be of great value in his performances on the clavicembalo. This keyboard instrument was, after all, related to the organ, both in regard to sound and in regard to technical requirements made of the performer. The tone of the clavicembalo, penetrating, clear, not easily modified, of silvery brightness, and of thrilling, festive character, offered unlimited possibilities both in regard to solo work and in regard to concerted performances. The clavichord, on the other hand, was used by Bach only because this was the sole instrument on which students could learn and achieve a dominating "cantabile" or singing style. As he himself said, he used it for study and for instruction because it was effective pedagogically "in the obtaining of a cantabile style in performance."

For Bach *clavier* always means first of all only the manual of a keyboard instrument, a term which includes the organ; in the final analysis it refers to the organ itself. In his compositions he uses the term *clavier* to designate the number of manuals; he does not, however, indicate whether he means an organ or a stringed keyboard instrument. When manuals are to be played separately, he gives the direction, "a 2 Clav." If a pedal keyboard is to be added, the direction reads: "a 2 Clav. e Pedale." Whenever the terms "pedaliter" or "con pedale" are used in church music, we are to understand that an organ is meant; when in chamber music, the references are to the pedal-clavicembalo or to the pedal-clavichord. For the proper performance of Bach's organ and clavier works, especially the later compositions, it is important to remember these facts.

Violinist in Weimar (1703)

Already as early as 1702 the young master had applied for a position as organist in Sangerhausen. His first appointment, however, did not take place until the next year. He was accepted as violinist at the court of Weimar, where his grandfather at one time had served as *Spielmann* and *musicus instrumentalis*. Here Bach heard the widely traveled violinist Johann Paul Westhoff. His achievements in double-stops and in improvising in several parts represent a high point in the violin technique of Central Germany.

Bach's patron, the young Duke Ernst of Sachsen-Weimar, a brother of the reigning duke, was not only a lover of music and a performer on the violin and the clavier; he was also active as a composer, and in addition enjoyed making adaptations of Italian concert music. Johann Gottfried Walther dedicated his book of instructions on the art of composition, a substantial and important work, to the young prince.

Organist in Arnstadt (1703—1707)

In the same year (1703) Bach removed to Arnstadt, to become organist at the newly built organ in the Bonifatiuskirche. From here he journeyed on foot to Lübeck, an undertaking which has gained considerable prominence in the story of his life. He set out to hear Dietrich Buxtehude, the sixty-six-year-old organist in the Marienkirche. In him Bach was to find his real master teacher. The creative power of Buxtehude's personality and his art so deeply

39

influenced Bach that he forgot to return to his post in Arnstadt. Guilty of serious violations of the stipulations that had governed his leave of absence, he came into violent conflict with his superiors.

After this personal meeting with Buxtehude, Bach, once again back in Arnstadt, began to be aware of his mastery also in the field of composition. "Here he really displayed the earliest fruits of his diligence in the art of organ playing and of composition," the necrology reports. "For the most part he had acquired this art only by studying the works of the famous and thoroughgoing composers of that time and by applying his own careful meditation to those works." Philipp Emanuel agrees with this verdict of the necrology concerning his father. He states that "even this one practice alone — his continual practice of meditating on the works of others — made a pure and strong contrapuntalist *(Fugisten)* of him already in his youth."

The masters of the art of fugue whom Bach had taken as exemplars, masters whom he "loved and studied," include (according to Philipp Emanuel), first of all, Gerolamo Frescobaldi. He was the oldest of them all. He was the creator of the baroque art of keyboard playing in Rome. Bach owned a complete copy of Frescobaldi's chief work, "Fiori musicali di diverse compositioni" (Venice, 1635). It represents a choice selection of toccatas and other pieces from the world of liturgical organ playing, all of them typical of form and sound prevailing in that era. Bach had copied this work himself and had marked it with his signature, "J. S. Bach 1714." In addition to Frescobaldi there were "several good old French masters," aside from the organists, associates of Couperin, who were active in Paris. This non-Paris group included, among others, Nicolaus de Grigny, organist at the Cathedral of Reims; Andre Raison, from whom Bach borrowed the theme of his organ Passacaglia; and Louis Marchand, organist at the court of Versailles. Marchand was one of the leading masters of the keyboard in his day; he had become famous through his improvisations, but was also sought and honored as a teacher. Bach's German contemporaries, older than Bach himself, included first of all the two leading pupils of Frescobaldi at the imperial court in Vienna, Johann Jakob Froberger and Kaspar Kerll, as well as Delphin Strungk, Reinken, Buxtehude, and Buxtehude's pupil Bruhns, and finally J. K. Ferdinand Fischer, Pachelbel, and Böhm.

Bach had gone even beyond this group of masters for influence and direction. From "far and near," as he himself says, and "not without cost" to himself, he had gathered "good, serviceable materials in the form of the choicest selections of church music," and had made copies of them. So long as a tradition prevailed which conformed to the principles of genuine art, music was learned by means of imitating and copying. The youthful creative imagination of Bach was beginning to be deeply stirred in just this way. The impluse, powerful and stimulating, was provided when he appropriated and studied works of German, Italian, and French origin, and also when he meditated on the art of con-

41

temporary and older masters. Self-evidently, his own productivity helped to develop his creative power.

True enough, his services on the Arnstadt organ often met with opposition on the part of the ducal consistory. The complaint was that "until the present time he has made many strange variations in the playing of the chorale, and has mingled it with foreign and improper tones, so that the congregation has become confused by what has been done." He was also confronted with the charge that "he had been playing too long; on the other hand, after he had received a notification from the superintendent in regard to this matter, he had gone immediately to the other extreme and cut his playing too short." Bach was furthermore accused of running counter to the prevailing practice governing the singing of women. Women were to be silent in church and in the music of the church. Even in opera, Bach was reminded by his superiors, feminine roles were taken by men. Bach, however, "had permitted a strange maiden to be in the choir loft and to make music there." The incident caused Mattheson to make the humorous comment that he had at first (ca. 1715) been emphatically told, under no circumstances to place female singers in the church in a position which would permit them to be seen by anyone; in the end, however, no one could see and hear them enough. The strange young woman, who was also the first female singer in the performance of Bach's church music, was the master's cousin, Maria Barbara, destined to be his life's companion. She was the youngest daughter of Johann Michael Bach, organist in Gehren. As a result, the wedding did not take place in Arnstadt but in nearby Dornheim. The marriage was solemnized on October 17, 1707, by a clergyman who was a friend of the master.

Organist in Mühlhausen (1707—1708)

Shortly before his marriage Bach had assumed his new position as organist of the Blasiuskirche in Mühlhausen. Here he was the successor of Johann Georg Ahle. Already after the passage of one year he exchanged this post for a new assignment.

Organist in Weimar (1708—1717)

Bach went to Weimar, to serve as court and chamber organist. In Mühlhausen Bach had taken a lively part in the discussions of ecclesiastical factions, particularly also because decisions in regard to the cultivation of church music were controlled by these parties. On the one side stood the representatives of old-Lutheran orthodoxy. They had a high regard for music. In the church service they gave a free hand to those who were interested in fostering the cause of music and permitted them to carry on activities of the widest scope. Their generous attitude was the result of the basic principles they held in regard to music: they believed music making to be a means of praising God and a sacrifice for the Creator, to proclaim His glory. On the other side the battle was waged by the followers of the new Pietistic movement. The members of this group had little insight into the merit of church music. They could not understand that the great, traditional works of church art possessed value as religious symbols, as expressions of faith. As a result, the members of this group sought more and more to place increasing restrictions on the use and cultivation of art in the church service.

For Bach there could be no question as to where he would stand in this battle. His position was on the side of music in the church, particularly because the dispute included questions in regard to the nature and purpose of music in the church. Bach felt compelled to oppose the chief pastor of his church in Mühlhausen, a Pietist. He was drawn with equal intensity to Pastor Eilmar, an orthodox minister of that town. Bach not only depended on Eilmar to furnish libretti for his first cantatas but also chose him as sponsor of his own son, Friedemann, the first-born.

All the turmoil of this dissension among ecclesiastical parties served only to make the youthful music master the more clearly convinced as to his true function. Both accuracy of perception and ripened intensity of feeling are reflected and revealed in a communication which came from Bach's hands under the date of January 25, 1708. The letter contained his request for release from his post at Mühlhausen. In sending the request, Bach declared this to be the ultimate purpose *(Endzweck)* of all his creative activity: to provide "regulated church music to the glory of God" *(eine regulierte Kirchenmusik zu Gottes Ehren).*

At this same time Georg Friedrich Händel was devoting himself to opera, thus finding his world and the spirit of his age in secular activity. Bach, on the other hand, bound music to the Great Commission of the church. He sought first of all to provide "well-conceived church music" *(wohlzufassende Kirchenmusik)*. Next, he hoped to "regulate" *(regulieren)* it; that is, to give music its true place, its ordered and ordering function, a position established by custom but also imposing high obligations on the incumbent. Thus Bach was using the term "regulated" in the same sense as did the ancient tradition which spoke of "regulated" canons and other clergymen in a cathedral or of choir leaders and the heads of monasteries. The term was used of those who still lived in the *vita canonica,* in the convent or conventlike order and community.

III

THE COMPOSER AND
MATURE PERFORMER

It is evident, then, that for Bach the terms "music" and "music making" *(Musizieren)* possessed a meaning which was in agreement with the tradition of German Lutheranism. According to this concept, the production of music, although indeed an artistic activity, does not proceed from the mere subjectivity of a religious experience or from the individualism of a pietistic emotion of the heart, nor is it to be aimed at the personal edification of a single person. Rather, it proceeds from an objective source: the Biblical revelation of the Word of God through Jesus Christ. Thus it proceeds from a source which is not only the foundation of the entire creative communion of believers, who constitute the church of Christ; this generating foundation also bears and binds all members in a common bond. And the sole aim of this music is the glory of God, the Creator and Lord — *ad majorem Dei gloriam.*

The first characteristic of that kind of music and music making is that it adheres to its source. In other words, it is bound to the word of the Bible, to church song, and to the chorale. Even the instrumental and secular music of Bach does not stand in any kind of intended contrast to this religio-ecclesiastical association or connection; in fact, its basic affinity is the same. This music, too, bears throughout the marks of a spiritual or at least a semispiritual quality.

FIRST PERIOD: ARNSTADT AND MUEHLHAUSEN (1703—1708)

This quality is evident in the first group of Bach's works (extending to the year 1708). This group consists of spiritual concerts (church cantatas), chorale partitas, preludes and fugues, toccatas, fantasias, organ chorales, sonatas, and capriccios; of the last group, one was composed "In honorem Joh. Christoph. Bachii" and another "For the departure of a most beloved brother" (Johann Jakob; he went to Poland first and then to Sweden, where he died as oboist in the service of Charles XII).

It is interesting to observe how in the last-named capriccio the emotions occasioned by the departure are protrayed musically in a style which imitates the Italian church sonata transcribed for clavier by Kuhnau. In the opening Arioso there are the "cajoling appeals of friends, who endeavor to dissuade the brother from undertaking the journey." In the following Andante the friends "picture various mishaps that might befall him in a strange land." The Adagissimo, based on a chromatic ostinato, brings "a universal lament of the friends" and concludes with the statement: "Since the friends see that it cannot, after all, be otherwise, they now come to bid the brother farewell." The final section brings an aria, in dancelike measures, and a fugue, portraying the postilion who gives the horn signal and cracks the whip. All these features are the marks of an imitative musical art of semispiritual character, patterned after the example submitted in Kuhnau's "Biblical Histories" for clavier.

The influence of Pachelbel and Böhm is similarly at work in Bach's chorale partitas for organ and in compositions of freer design. In the partita on the Passion hymn "Sei gegrüsst, Jesu gütig," Bach employs a highly significant device. The chorale, which is not only the cantus firmus but also symbol of purity of doctrine, is contrasted with independent voices, not dependent for their content or substance on the heritage of the chorale. These voices, lyric in character, are to depict the emotions of the human heart. The combination of these two contrasting elements represents a type of organ chorale preludes which was to reach its culmination in Bach's later works.

Thus the instrumental compositions of Bach make the first and most dependable disclosure in regard to his creativeness and its underlying feeling of strength and power. These compositions show that the origin of his individual style is to be found in his indebtedness to the musical heritage of his tribe. At the same time his creative power reveals itself also in his vocal compositions; here he is continually making new efforts and new attempts.

48

True enough, instrumental music at first dominates even in the total sum of the church cantatas of Bach. When Bach was young, the development of the church cantata had brought it to a point in the road at which it was confronted with the necessity of a choice between motet and spiritual concert. The early cantatas of Bach are dominated, first of all, by music forms which had been current among the older town musicians; this material is used for introductions and interludes. Prominent also are imitations of instrumental forms which are then used in choruses and arias. Another conspicuous element is represented by the solo passages which are closely related to spiritual songs. The use of these various materials results in a structure rich in contrasts.

This same dependence on the traditional music of performance is seen also in the unsingable vocal parts, which depersonalize the human voice and give it a purely instrumental character. In general, the lyrical passages composed by the youthful Bach bear a strong resemblance to instrumental music.

The texts of the cantatas consist of Bible verses, stanzas of church hymns, and a few verses of original poetry. The manner in which they are set to music resembles the style of the accompanied ariosi of Schütz and Buxtehude.

Concerning the manner in which his father set texts to music, Ph. Emanuel declared: "He worked devoutly and was governed strictly by the content of the words. He refused to be guilty of a ludicrous rejection of the words; nor would he limit his attention to only a few words and then neglect to

express the entire sense or meaning of the passage —
a practice that gives birth to strange and ridiculous
thoughts but nonetheless occasionally moves certain
people to wonderment and admiration, not merely
ignorant people but also some who pretend to have
understanding in these matters." It is a fact that
when Bach provides music for a text he does much
more than to consider individual words and pictures.
With the attitude of a simple believer, he sinks
himself deeply into a contemplation of the entire
subject matter presented by the religious content of
the text.

Bach's art in his early cantatas finds poetic expression in the arioso passages, accompanied as they
are by instruments and placed in a framework of
instrumental music. This instrumental accompaniment interprets the total spiritual message and emotion which the Biblical text was intended to convey.
Another means employed by Bach for the same purpose is his artistic treatment of the chorale.

In this mode of procedure Bach allies himself
directly with the tradition of the seventeenth century.
When he employs new devices, innovations originat-
ing in the world of opera, he does so only with the
greatest of care.

As a result, when we observe the artistic treatment of the chorale in other church cantatas of
Bach's day, we discover a most important contrast.
Even in the works of masters like Telemann and
Graun the treatment of the chorale not only becomes superficial and shallow but is increasingly
neglected. Bach, on the other hand, is careful to
have his cantatas continue the traditional art of

50

chorale treatment. In fact, he gives ever greater prominence to the chorale until finally, in his later chorale cantatas, the chorale occupies the central position.

The earliest cantata of Bach which has been handed down to us in its original form — and the only one of his compositions published with parts in Bach's own lifetime — is the cantata *God Is My King*. Entitled "Congratulatory Church Motet" *(Glückwünschende Kirchen-Motette)*, it was written for the election of a new town council in Mühlhausen in 1708. Bach composed a second cantata of a similar nature *(Ratsstück)* in the next year, but it has not been found.

The cantata was presented after the sermon in the festival service with which the official year of the new council was begun. The text consists of passages from the Psalms and of other verses from the Old Testament; in addition, it contains a chorale stanza and several rhymed verses paying homage to God as omnipotent Governor, to the new city government, and to Emperor Joseph I. The rhymed tribute was prepared either by Bach himself or by Pastor Eilmar.

The opening section of the cantata achieves structure by means of a six-part ensemble, three divisions of which are concertizing instrumental choruses. The cantata begins with a ripieno chorus which has a characteristically baroque heaping of words in the opening line: "God, God — God is my King of old."

This section is followed by an arioso duet, "Aria con Corale in Canto," written in the form of an organ

51

chorale. In this duet an accompanying organ bass is provided for the statement by the tenor, "I am now eighty years old." The words of the tenor, however, are contrasted with the prayer sung by the soprano voice. The prayer consists of the sixth stanza of the chorale, "O God, Thou Faithful God!" It ends with the plea:

> Thy patience on me shed,
> Avert all sin and shame,
> And crown my hoary head
> With honor free from blame.[2]

What is musically significant in this duet is that it expresses a contrast which is true to life. On the one hand we have Christian faith in Him who is the Lord of life and death. On the other hand we have a reference to the fact that human beings grow old and must die. But it is just this latter phenomenon which is questioned by the objective tone of the chorale. This contrast is developed further by a four-voice a cappella fugue, "As thy days, so shall thy strength be, and God will be with thee in whatsoever thou doest." The fugue provides the transition to the homage heard in the bass aria, "The day is Thine, and the night also," written over an ostinato bass. This transitional influence of the fugue extends also to the subsequent alto aria, "Thy mighty power preserves our borders," and to the closing chorus. This final number, hailing "the new government," once again unites all the tonal ensemble utilized in the opening section; the middle portion brings a choral fugue dedicated to the Emperor.

---

[2] *The Lutheran Hymnal*, No. 395. Translation copyrighted in 1941 by Concordia Publishing House, St. Louis, Mo.

The similarity of structure in the Cantata *God's Time Is Best* reveals an affinity and relationship of spirit with that of the cantata *God Is My King.* Known as *Actus tragicus* the cantata was probably composed on the occasion of the death of Bach's uncle Tobias Lämmerhirt (1707).

The cantata begins with a sonatina marked "Molto adagio." Two *Blockflöten* and two viols di gamba, whose themes are placed over a figured bass, console the mourning congregation with a wordless proclamation of Gospel comfort.

After several sections differing from one another as to time, tempo, and key, we come to the major contrast in the cantata. First the musical symbolism depicts the inexorable law of the Old Testament: "It is the old decree — Man, thou must die." This announcement is made in ancient style, in strictly fugal form, by the three lower voices of the chorus. By way of striking contrast two flutes announce the chorale "To God I have committed all" ("Ich hab' mein' Sach' Gott heimgestellt"). Even in its wordless form, this contrasting declaration of faith was recognized by the congregation. The contrast is intensified by the fact that the boy sopranos sing a passage from the Revelation of St. John: "Yea, come — yea, come, Lord Jesus, come!" This plea, coming in utter simplicity from the children of God, is an expression of the believers' trust and confidence.

At this point followed the funeral sermon of the pastor. Thereupon the alto soloist turns to Jesus with the prayer of faith: "Into Thy hands I commend my spirit." The voice of Jesus, heard in a bass setting, replies: "Today shalt thou be with Me in Paradise." After several measures a chorale is heard over the words of Jesus. The alto section of the chorus sings Luther's death and burial hymn, "In peace and joy I now depart."

The final section brings a four-part setting of the last stanza in the chorale "In Thee, Lord, have I put my trust." [3] In its choice of key and also in its structure this closing section recalls the opening sonatina. It directs the attention of the congregation to that which is universally binding on all those who would lead the Christian life: membership in the church and the duty to glorify the Lord of the church: "All glory, praise, and majesty to Father, Son, and Spirit be!" This section concludes with a solemn ending: "Through Jesus Christ. Amen."

What we find in these early works of the master — and this is typical of every department of his creative activity — can hardly be called a definite position or individualism in regard to style, nor do we find a direct and uncomplicated line of development. Rather, we observe in Bach a certain difficulty in deciding upon a choice of the materials that lay at hand ready for use. With a kind of stormy eagerness he had seized upon examples and patterns from every available source. Now these examples and patterns lay before him in their intricate and involved diversity. Moreover, their style involved certain basic assumptions. It was no easy task for Bach to adopt these various types, to imitate them, and to make

[3] *The Lutheran Hymnal*, No. 524:7.

54

them fruitful agents for the discovery of his own creative powers.

Bach did not really discover his true basic strength as a creative artist until he became organist at the court in Weimar. He had obtained his first position in Weimar five years previously; now, in 1708, he returned. The Necrology states: "The pleasure and approving delight which his gracious Excellency displayed toward his playing spurred him on to do everything possible to gain the mastery in the art of organ playing. Moreover, here in Weimar he wrote most of his organ compositions."

From Weimar Bach became known throughout the musical world. From here his fame spread as the greatest performer, teacher, and composer of organ music in Germany. He was invited everywhere and was consulted for his opinion when tests or estimates of new or rebuilt organs were needed. Students from far and near streamed to him in Weimar and sought his guidance.

The master of the organ is described in the following words of Philipp Emanuel:

No one has ever tested organs as he has done. He combined unrelenting sharpness with the utmost integrity. His understanding of organ construction was thorough and of the highest order. If an organ builder had done honest work and had suffered loss or some other disadvantage in the process of building, my father induced the employers to allow a reimbursement.

No one understood organ registration as well as he. Organists often became terrified when he wished to play their organ and when he began selecting stops according to his own preference. They imagined that his choice of stops could not possibly sound good; later, however, they heard the result of his combinations and were astounded. This expert knowledge and proficiency died with him.

His first act in testing an organ was to say humorously: "Above all things I must know whether the organ has good lungs." To determine the answer, he drew every speaking stop and made the greatest possible effort to play full organ. At this point the organ builders would often become pale with fright.

His chief concern in the supervision of his instruments and also of the entire orchestra was purity of tone and accuracy of pitch. No one could tune his instruments to please him, or quill them (a term which has reference to cutting the quills for the cembalo, or *Kielflügel*). He did everything himself.

According to this report Bach had gone far beyond the knowledge and ability of the organ builders and organists of his time. Although their skill was considerable and not to be despised, he excelled in all questions concerning the construction of instruments, temperament, tuning, and building acoustics, and especially in regard to the numerous and manifold skills involved in the art of organ building, arranging, and registration.

It was characteristic of him that he himself designed the plan for the rebuilding of the organ he had played in Mühlhausen and that he supervised the execution of the plans from Weimar. The following specification was used (1709):

56

Hauptwerk

Quintaden	16′	Nasat	2⅔′
Fagott	16′	Oktave	2′
Prinzipal	8′	Sesquialtera	II
Viola da gamba	8′	Mixtur	IV
Oktave	4′	Zimbel	II
Gedackt	4′	(Glockenspiel)	

Brustwerk

Stillgedackt	8′	Oktave	2′
Schallmei	8′	Terz	1⅗′
Zartflöte	4′	Mixtur	III
Quinte	2⅔′		

Rückpositiv

Quintaden	8′	Spitzflöte	2′
Gedackt	8′	Sesquialtera	II
Prinzipal	4′	Quintflöte	1⅓′
Salizional	4′	Zimbel	III
Oktave	2′		

Pedal

Untersatz	32′	Trompete	8′
Prinzipal	16′	Oktave	4′
Subbasz	16′	Kornett	2′
Posaune	16′	Rohrflöte	1′
Oktave	8′	Mixtur	IV

Accessories

Tremulant
Coupler: Brustwerk to Hauptwerk
Coupler: Hauptwerk to Pedal
Zimbelstern and Pauke

In Weimar Bach performed on an organ which had been designed by Ludwig Compenius, who died in Erfurt in 1671. In 1647 Compenius had constructed the great organ in the Predigerkirche of Erfurt for Johann Bach and Pachelbel. He was a friend of Samuel Scheidt and was acquainted with the style of organ building prevailing in the Netherlands. The organ which he constructed in 1657 in the Weimar Castle Church, the so-called *Himmelsburg,* was built into the space between the upper gallery and the ceiling of the church, and for that reason had no *Rückpositiv.* In Bach's day the organ had the following specification:

Hauptwerk

Quintaden	16′	Oktave	4′
Prizipal	8′	Mixtur	VI
Gembshorn	8′	Zimbel	III
Grobgedackt	8′	Glockenspiel	
Quintaden	4′		

Brustwerk

Prinzipal	8′	Gedackt	4′
Viola da gamba	8′	Oktave	4′
Gedackt	8′	Waldflöte	2′
Trompete	8′	Sesquialtera	IV
		in octave	

Pedal

Untersatz	32′	Prinzipal	8′
Subbasz	16′	Trompete	8′
Posaune	16′	Kornett	4′
Violenbasz	16′		

Accessories

Tremulant
Coupler: Pedal to Manual
Coupler: Brustwerk to Hauptwerk
Zimbelstern

If we compare the two organs according to their tonal design, we can form a conception of the ideal which Bach had in mind at this time (in distinction from later years) in regard to the tonal realization of his organ music. We see that Bach's ideal of organ tone was rooted deeply in the artistic tradition of the great organ builders of Central Germany. It is to be distinguished just as sharply from the tonal ideal represented in the organs designed by Gottfried Silbermann as from the ideal found in the Hanseatic organs; the latter group moved Bach to admiration particularly because of their rich supply of reed stops.

The distinction becomes even clearer when, by way of further comparison, we add the tonal character of the last organ which Bach, together with Silbermann on September 26, 1746, examined and approved: it is the work of Zacharias Hildebrandt, a pupil of Silbermann, in the City Church of Naumburg along the Saale River. An examination of this organ will help us to arrive at the principles that Bach held.

From the baroque organ he took over the grouped arrangement of organ registration, classifying the equipment in tonally related "choirs." He also incorporated the *Werkcharakter* of the *plena* of the individual clavier, even when the number of stops was relatively small. In a manner corresponding to the tonally related instrumental choirs of his orchestra, Bach essentially retained the choirs of principals with their narrow scale and strength of tone, the flutes and horns with their wide range and fullness of tone, the reeds with their typical "snarling" *(schnarrend)*, and the solo stops. He granted less independence to the choir of wide range than to the choir of narrow range; he enlarges the pedal with a grave *(gravitätischem)* tone, so that it may serve not only as bass clavier but also as *cantus firmus* clavier.

Thus the Weimar Compenius organ of Bach has the separated voices of those sections that are bearers of the *cantus firmus:* trumpets, cornets, sesquialtera, and cymbal. It also has a "werkhaft durchgebaut" pedal section, whose brilliant power and fullness may have inspired the master to engage in the festal upsurge of the pedal solos in the preludes and toccatas that belong to his Weimar period.

The suggestions for registration contained in Bach's organ music also find their fulfillment in both the Mühlhausen and the Weimar organs. In addition, however, Bach was aware of the fact that assignments of a new kind had been given to the organ. These new assignments had arisen in conjunction with the execution of figured bass in concertizing music and because of the organ's responsibility to lead congregational singing in the church service. From the very beginning, therefore, Bach strove to soften the heterogeneous variety of color afforded by organ registration; to bring the various choirs of organ stops together in an assimilation and conformity based on range and tone; and to unify them in such a manner as to make it possible to group them, around the main choir of principals, as secondary choirs and as accompanying choirs of the figured bass.

By this tonal improvement of the organ Bach also enabled the principle of the concerto and the concertizing style of music (with tutti and soli, ripieno and concerto) to assert itself. For that reason he was pleased to find that in the new style of organ construction the stops that were related in structure and tone were grouped together in sets of several octaves on one and the same clavier. He also hailed the utilization of string registration that had a fine, singing tone. He welcomed devices which would make the organ more readily responsive to shading against a background of a more deeply darkened organ tone. He was delighted with the possibility of merging and mixing the tone colors.

One reason for the notable advance Bach made in the science and art of the organ was the substantial help he received in Weimar from Joh. Gottfried Walther of Erfurt. Walther was not only Bach's contemporary, cousin, and friend, but was related to him by a spiritual kinship. For the space of one year Walther had been serving as organist of the City Church in Weimar.

In 1714 Bach became concertmaster at the court in Weimar. He had previously declined an invitation to become the successor of Händel's teacher, Friedrich Zachow, in Halle and to serve there as organist and director of music in the Liebfrauenkirche. "The obligations connected with this assignment consisted chiefly in the composition and presentation of church music." (Necrology.) In the meantime Bach was striving for an attractive post like the one held by Georg Philipp Telemann, who was master of chamber music at the court in Eisenach. To obtain a position of that kind Bach forced his employers to release him from serving in Weimar. In 1717 he went to Köthen, where he became master of chamber music at the court of his friend, Count Leopold.

The same year was to witness the memorable contest between Bach and Marchand, the former court organist of Versailles. It was to take place at the electoral court of Saxony in Dresden. Here, under the influence of August the Strong, the presentation of Italian opera, chamber music, church music, and French instrumental music had reached a high degree of perfection.

Actually, as is well known, the competitive encounter between the two musicians was never held. Although the Frenchman enjoyed a good reputation in his day, he decamped and abandoned the field. By this turn of events, however, Bach secured a priceless trophy for his countrymen: the evident superiority of German music over the art of the Romance countries. Bach was now on the way to achieve greatness as an organist, not only for himself but also for the entire age in which he lived. By means of his productivity Germany was reaching cultural maturity and was becoming the artistic center of Europe.

The courts of the German princes in Bach's day were permeated by a spirit that was essentially different from the one that prevailed in the circle of cantors, organists, and town musicians. A so-called "mixed standard" had triumphed at the courts. It was the stylistic ideal of Europe, based on the principle of the concerto. It succeeded in blending Italian, French, and German styles into a higher unity. This fusion took place not so much in church music as in compositions of chamber music, opera, and ballet. In these art forms composers manifested a decided preference for *Welsch,* i. e., for Italian and French, music.

This à la mode taste for the current fashion set the standard in the musical life at the small German courts. It found expression in the entire realm of art forms existing in Italian opera and French ballet and their new methods in regard to theater and orchestra; it found expression also in what had become the leading form of orchestral composition: the overture "a la française," with its sequence (suite) of dances portraying a certain role or vogue; it found expression furthermore in sonatas and in secular cantatas in settings for small groups *(alla camera);* and last but not least, it found expression in the dominating musical art form of the day: the Italian concerto.

The new musical trend revealed significant personal traits. It was a mirror, vividly reflecting the narrow but intense absolutism of petty princes, their hunger for power, their eagerness to show that they were meeting the requirements of their social station, their desire for a cosmopolitan way of living. All these were responsible factors in the blinding brilliance of the new sensuousness and the transitory glamor found in various compositions: in dramatic works portraying human emotions on an operatic stage; in the emotionalism of suggestive rhythms and the compact instrumental polyphony of French overtures; in the elegance of variegated suites consisting of minuets, bourrees, passepieds, gavottes, and rondos; in the surfeiting euphony of Italian chamber music, in the delicate bel canto of their instrumental melodies, in the sweet and cloying consonance of their music for violin, clavier, and vocal solos.

The spirit of this courtly musical life reaches its climax in the concerto. This art form made possible a dramatic exchange between orchestra (as tutti, ripieno, cappella, concerto grosso) and the ensemble of soloists (as concerto piccolo) or the soloist, and also between the larger and smaller groups of concerto and ripieno players.

To achieve leadership in this area of courtly life and its art of unbounded fantasy, only one course could be followed: the way leading to the youthful movement of musical art in the Romance countries, especially in Italy. It is the road that Bach chose. Although he himself never visited Italy, he approached the young Italian art of Torelli, Corelli, Albinoni, Vivaldi, and Scarlatti with virtually unequaled enthusiasm, open-mindedness, and willingness.

The overwhelming abundance of stimulating suggestions flowing in upon Bach like a torrential stream from the great wealth of Italian concert and chamber music formed a new treasure which Bach made his own. Significantly, in taking possession of this material, Bach again worked as an artist of the keyboard, especially of the organ. He provided transcriptions and revisions; in doing so, he dealt freely with his basic materials, not hesitating to develop them further or to impose new forms on the Italian prototypes.

What Bach did was a repetition of the ancient practice of craftsmen who had gone before him:

he learned by imitating the design and workmanship of others. But how much more beneficially this process operated on Bach's mental faculties than on those of Telemann, who also was engaged in imitating and improving French and Italian models! How mightily the unique and incomparable creative powers of Bach were stirred by what he found!

In his Weimar organ compositions, the regularity of form and setting that had shackled the Italian types was broken by the force of a new freedom which was at work within the framework of the structure that Bach had taken over. Even in respect to purely formal considerations we dare not overlook the fact that these organ works of Bach's Weimar period provide a variety of solutions that are as self-wrought and original as they are definitive and final.

The lyrical, cantabile quality of Italian violin themes is transformed into organ themes of strict design, carefully observing counterpoint and motifs. The thin, delicate, high tone is given a new setting, imparting solidity, weight, and depth; it is divested of tonal beauty which is appealing only because it is obvious or which is limited to the immediately striking. Parts that had moved freely and independently are blended together in a firmly constructed, dynamic whole, possessing a stern severity of strength, powerful through intensity of tone and movement.

We must remember, however, that the questions which pressed in upon Bach in regard to the new musical treasures at the Weimar court were by no means restricted to considerations of style and form.

The questions confronting him dealt also with the new musical public and the new attitude toward music. Sociological changes, involving reclassifications, had created a new type of audience and a new appraisal of musical activity.

Until the time of his service at the Weimar court, all of Bach's creative work had been intended solely for listeners who, for lack of a better designation, might be called church people *(Kirchenvolk)*. The term is a general one, representing various strata of cultural development and varying levels of musical receptivity. This larger group was now supplemented by the "little" circles gathered at the courts of petty princes — small groups of connoisseurs and dilettanti *(Kenner* und *Liebhaber)*. They were known for a particularly friendly and open-minded attitude toward the independent world of art forms.

In its attitude toward music the new circle of listeners had developed a point of view which was entirely different from the one commonly found among bourgeois organists and town musicians. The attempt to fit the old bourgeois music culture, in which Bach had been reared, to courtly, worldly, and "enlightened" standards had developed and produced a new ideal. It was the ideal of a "musician beloved by God and the world and therefore richer and more fortunate than other persons." Even though "he might not be rewarded in proportion to his merits," he would, according to Kuhnau, "nevertheless enjoy a foretaste of heavenly pleasure and would ultimately be ushered into the castle of heaven owned by our great God Himself."

The ideal created by this new bourgeois group, the ideal of the "fortunate musician" *(Ideal des glueckseligen Musicus),* represents an endeavor to adapt ancient standards to new conditions. The old tradition, binding music and musicians to ecclesiastical and religious activity, was to be brought into a harmonious relationship with the demands of world and time. On one occasion Bach himself expressed this thought. While teaching his pupils, he dictated a sentence which has since become well known. "As in the case of all music, so also thorough bass should have no other purpose or final reason than this: it should exist only for the glory of God and the recreation of the human spirit. Where this point is not carefully observed, there will be no real music, but only a devilish clamor and monotony." In this statement the work of giving delight to the human spirit assumes a position next to that of praising God and is equally justified with it. This juxtaposition is not undertaken, however, without adding a richly instructive supplementary thought, like the one that Bach expresses on the title page of his *Orgelbüchlein.* That book was to serve a twofold purpose:

> To give all praise to God on high,
> While men might teach themselves thereby.

> (Dem höchsten Gott allein zu Ehren,
> Dem Nächsten draus sich zu belehren.)

Musicians in Bach's day sought to find the meaning and essence of music in a hidden numerical order and design, as set forth by Leibniz in his well-known definition of music (1712). Leibniz was a descendant of an old generation of organists in Saxony. His great-grandfather, Christoph Leibniz, had been organist in Pirna at the Elbe River. In reply to the question: "What, after all, is it that enables music to give pleasure?" Leibniz supplies the following answer: "Musica est exercitium arithmeticae occultum nescientis se numerare animi," i. e., Music is a hidden arithmetical exercise of the human soul, which performs this process of numbering unconsciously. A similar statement concerning music was made by Johann Gottfried Walther when he dedicated his work on the art of composition to the Duke of Weimar. Walther called music "a living picture of good order and a loving mother of many pleasures" (1708). A related spirit is observable in the rhymed verse of Joh. Christoph Lorber, the royal poet at the court of Weimar. In his "Praise of the Noble Art of Music," Lorber provides a series of profound couplets to show that the value of music is observable on two levels: one, heavenly; another, mundane. Lorber says that the correctness of this view becomes apparent in the light of the Christian faith concerning divine revelation and creation.

> Du aber, edle Kunst! Der Seligkeit bemerk',
> Du Kind der Ewigkeit, du himmlisch Wunderwerk,
> Der Engel Eigentum, die von dem ew'gen Lichte
> Vor Gottes Majestät, vor Gottes Angesichte
> Ihr allerheiligst Lied, das noch kein Menschen Mund,
> Hervorzubringen weisz, das keinem Ohre kund
> Gemachet werden kann, mit Engelstimmen singen,
> Bleibst himmlisch, wie du bist; der Mensch zwar mag dich zwingen
> Durch die Erfindungskunst zu seiner Möglichkeit,

Die sich zum Wunder macht, doch der Vollkommenheit
Noch weit entfernt ist. Zu Gottes Lob und Preise
Gehört ein himmlisch Lied, der Engel heil'ge Weise.
In solcher Herrlichkeit, in solchem Heiligtum
Führt die Musik sich auf: ihr überird'scher Ruhm
Fühlt nichts Vergängliches . . .
Die ganze Wesenheit des Weltgebäudes steht
Mit dir in Kompagnie. Wo sich Saturnus dreht,
Wo Föbus' Schwester uns ihr blasses Silber zeiget,
Wo sich der Erdenball zu seinem Mittel neiget,
Da regt sich deine Kraft. Dies alles ist erbaut
Nach deiner Harmonie. Wer deinen Lehrern traut,
Wer ihrer Schüler sich bedient, wer nicht gewöhnet,
Dasz er ein jedes Ding verachtet und verhöhnet,
Was ihm in Kopf nicht will: der stimmet mir itzt bei
Und zeiget, dasz der Mensch ganz musikalisch sei.

Here the elements of a comprehensive inter-
pretation of music, derived from the spirit of old
Lutheranism and rejecting all rationalizing skepti-
cism, are placed in conflict with the philosophy of
music gaining currency in the new era of enlightenment and rationalism. Music, appearing as a "mir-
acle of heaven" (himmlisches Wunderwerk), engages
in the praise of God and stands in close connection
with the order prevailing in the entire universe.
This connection with universal order extends from
God and the world to man, who detects it from
within through experiences made possible by a hidden perceptive capacity of reason, a capacity which
is ranked equally with the certainty resulting from
religious faith. Why? Because the processes of
eternal law and order, which govern the physical,
moral, and artistic external world of man, are the
very same as those that reveal themselves to man
in his internal world. Thus the musicality of man's

being, both according to body and soul, becomes a symbol of God's creative work or of the harmony of the universe (the latter of these two being nothing else than a secularized name for creation). Theologian, philosopher, and musician live and work according to the same basic order and principle.

Fully awakened to a consciousness of his accountability to himself and to freedom in the midst of dependence, the "fortunate musician" *(glückseliger Musicus)* undertakes a momentous task: by means of his sovereign activity as a musician and his self-sufficient work as an artist he endeavors to imitate the creative work of God. His instrumental and vocal music achieves a high rank: it becomes an image of the divine order in creation. In his strong ties to ecclesiastical and religious life, in his Lutheranism marked by loyalty to confessional writings — in these we must, in the final analysis, find the compelling and decisive reasons why the "fortunate musician" could not be shaken by the ridicule of "enlightened" persons or by the pseudo-psychological acumen of rationalizing criticism. These are the reasons, too, why he escaped a danger that threatened him in his materials: he did not succumb to the trend that sought enlightenment, liberalism, and progress through foreign importations breathing the spirit of Romance countries.

At the end of his Weimar period and at the beginning of his years of service in Köthen Bach regarded himself as a musician of that kind, a "fortunate musician." He had reached the pinnacle in his life and work as well as in the mastery of his art. He was living in the sunshine of princely favor.

He was enjoying the friendship of earthly sovereigns — men who possessed, in addition to political importance, an understanding of music. He was surrounded by a group of enthusiastic pupils. Endowed with the rich gifts of a genius, he was, in addition, now in full possession of his youthful powers.

All of this is shown in the picture of Bach from this period. It shows the master of chamber music in his role at court. It reflects his open-mindedness to the things of this world and his joy of being; his sunny disposition and happiness; his optimism, the optimism of a man of good breeding and of good cheer.

SECOND PERIOD: WEIMAR (1708—1717)

A second group of masterworks (up to 1717) constitutes the harvest of the Weimar years. It consists chiefly of organ music and church cantatas. The unbroken delight in performance *(Spielfreude)* observable in the organ compositions achieves maturity in two respects: in the extent of form in the ground plan, achieved by carefully planning the movement of the harmonies, and in the greatness of the tonal range of its fantasy, achieved by the stepwise ordering of concerted solo and tutti groups and echo effects. These fantasias, toccatas, great and little preludes and fugues, and certainly the *Passacaglia and Fugue in C Minor* (1716), take rank among the products of the musical imagination of all times and nations as art works of undisputed greatness.

An examination of the structural basis underlying the *Passacaglia for Organ* will reveal the role

71

performed in Bach's extra-ecclesiastical works by the symbolizing power of numbers and the adherence to numbers as a metaphysical ground plan and basic movement in music. Already the favorableness of the theme gives us a "living picture of good order," regardless of which aspect we consider. We find a uniform change from arsis to thesis, which in itself provides both brevity and length; the rise from unaccented to accented position in alternations of major and minor seconds; the framework provided for the slow dance steps by an ascending step of a fifth at the beginning and a symmetrically corresponding descending step of a fourth at the close.

Here we can point out only briefly and in outline how the proportions of the theme influence the structural plan of the whole and how they succeed in binding and ordering the master's most daring powers of imagination. Of the twenty variations in the *Passacaglia*, based on a theme which recurs twenty times as basso ostinato, Variations 1, 2, 3—5, 6—9, and then also 12—15, 16—18, and 19 and 20 are bound together by means of common rhythmic "figures" in groups of 2, 3, 4 and 4, 3, 2 variations. In the two middle variations, Nos. 10 and 11, these chains of rhythmical figures are united with the theme by means of the double counterpoint in the octave. In this way the theme moves from the bass into the upper part and from there (in broken form) through the alto and tenor back into the bass. Here it returns, in the 16th variation, in its original position and form.

This strict grouping of the variations is founded on a valid law of proportion. According to this law simple numerical proportions determine the relation not only of the harmonic series in the musical concordances but also the relationship of the number of measures in the parts of the dance movements of the Bach clavier suites. Just as the relationship of the numbers *(Schwingungszahlen)* 1:2 yields the octave, 2:3 the fifth, 3:4 the fourth, etc., so a similar proportion n: (n plus 1) prevails in the number of measures of the second *(Reprise)* part, whose dance movements are a counterpart of the first section. Thus 16 measures of the first part correspond to 32 measures of the second part as 1:2, or 16:24 as 2:3, or 12:16 as 3:4, etc. In such "harmonic" numbers and numerical relationships we find mirrored the living unity of the process of the work. We note the ordered manner in which the development causes all parts to correspond to each other and to fit the whole.

The same structural plan for a series of variations bound to a theme in the bass forms the basis of the famous Chaconne in D Minor for solo violin (ca. 1720). An ostinato serves as the tonal scaffolding and foundation. A similar procedure is observable in the thirty "alterations" *(Veränderungen)* — ten groups of three variations each, with an introduction, a two-voiced episode for two claviers ("a 2 Clav."), a concluding canon, and finally a *quodlibet.* These variations are developed on the basis of a four-part ostinato in an aria contained in the *Notebook* for Anna Magdalena Bach. In 1742 the master composed these for one of his most gifted clavier pupils. His name was Johann Gottlieb

73

Goldberg. The composition is now known as the *"Goldberg Variations."*

This unity in Bach's art works that belong to the period of his early stylistic maturity in Weimar finds a threefold musical expression. It receives its rhythmical form in the unity of "figure," its melodic form in the unity of "motif," and its expressional form in the unity of "emotion" *(Affekt)*. Transferred to the chief forms of Bach's (and his contemporaries') instrumental music, the phenomenon is observable in the following manner: the composition of a suite achieves the form of its development from the unity of the measure (double or triple); the composition of a sonata achieves the form of its development from the unity of the tempo (slow or fast); the section of a partita (chorale-, song-, or dance-variation) achieves the form of its development from the unity of the time values prevailing in its body of figures (long or short note values).

In addition to organ compositions the Weimar period gives increasing prominence to the church cantata, a form employing, besides Scripture text and church hymn, the madrigal texts of two Lutheran court preachers — Erdmann Neumeister, of Weissenfels, and Salomo Franck, of Weimar. With these texts the older motetlike forms of instrumental introductory and episodic compositions, of aria-song with its instrumental ritornello, of arioso and chorale adaptations are joined by the forms of drama as found in the world of Neapolitan opera: the secco recitative, the three-divisional da capo-aria with *concertante* instrumental accompaniment. The Neumeister collection of libretti, from which Bach

74

drew heavily, had received the following title from Neumeister himself: "Spiritual Cantatas Instead of Church Music" (*Geistliche Kantaten statt einer Kirchenmusik* — 1704). In his Preface, Neumeister adds the comment: "If I were to give a brief description, I would say that a cantata is not unlike a section of an opera, composed of recitatives and arias."

With this development the way had been prepared for that secularization of church art which transformed church music into the religious cantata and the oratorio. Moreover, by using the musical form of the "spiritual concert" (*geistliches Konzert*), this development was destined to lead out of the church into the concert hall and the theater, out of the congregational service to an "enlightened" and merely "moral" public which, living beyond the confines of church and confessional documents, had no other religious needs than those that could be satisfied by a religion based on emotions and on nature.

This penetration of church music with the essential and characteristic elements of the "theatrical" style was vigorously attacked by Pietists. It was defended by Neumeister, the Lutheran cleric at court. He pointed to its instrumental character, which, he said, is equally available to spiritual and to worldly activities. But the new development had directed the creation of musical forms toward a way at whose end gleams the light of a musical ideal as found in Gluck operas and Haydn oratorios.

Treading this road, Bach of Weimar appears as one who, with unheard-of boldness, prepared the way for musical classicism and romanticism. His was a road which began with old-Lutheran church music and led on to the spiritual domains of Lutheran mysticism in early Pietism, disclosed by Buxtehude. It was a road pursued farther and with great success by Sebastian Bach's sons Johann Christian and Philipp Emanuel, who arrived at the threshold of the art of Mozart, Haydn, and Beethoven.

The sounds of an emotion, lyrical and subjective in character, break in upon Bach's Weimar church cantatas with a rich spiritual intensity and inwardness found elsewhere only in works by Buxtehude. This rapturous love of Jesus, this homesickness for heaven, this emotionally charged hope of a coming resurrection, this intensive longing and looking forward to the Last Judgment and the return of the Lord, as expressed in the cantatas, *I Had Much Distress in My Heart* (*Ich hatte viel Bekümmernis in meinem Herzen* — 1714), *Come, Sweet Hour of Death* (*Komm, du süsse Todesstunde* — 1715), *The Heavens Laugh, the Earth Rejoices* (*Der Himmel lacht, die Erde jubilieret* — 1715), *Watch and Pray, Pray and Watch!* (*Wachet, betet, betet, wachet!* — 1716) — all these qualities consolidate themselves into a picture of Bach, the mystic. It is a picture which, it would seem, can only with difficulty be harmonized with the distinctive traits of firm and solid Lutheran orthodoxy in the life and work of the master.

We need only hear the wonderful final chorale of the Easter cantata, *The Heavens Laugh.* Already the setting of the melody — a melody characterized by a noble importunity — is unusually high. Now this melody is solemnly transfigured by the bright radiance cast over it by the trumpet which, together

76

with the first violin, ascends into the highest regions of tone in a bold upsurge of soaring melody that towers over the chorale and shines upon it. "Thus mounts my soul to Jesus Christ." ("So fahr ich hin zu Jesu Christ." — Last stanza of the chorale "When my last hour is close at hand," *The Lutheran Hymnal*, No. 594.) Here we have an instance of the noblest kind of Lutheran mysticism in the music of Bach.

And yet the enthusiasm of this graphic description and eager anticipation of the hour of death, this ardent surrender to the last hour, this lingering at death's border of time and eternity, this sinking of oneself into the "evening of the world" (a concept which is then taken over into the affairs of everyday life) — all these belong to the basic eschatological content of Christian living and to the Christian doctrine of justification by faith, a doctrine made the more understandable to each individual person as a result of cross and affliction, of sin, death, and the devil.

This Lutheran faith, focused on grace, death, and eternity, no doubt finds its purest expression in the Passion of Christ. The Passion embraces the whole of Christian faith and touches its deepest emotion; the church year, with its miracles of Christmas, Easter, and Pentecost, is built around the Passion of Christ; the Passion serves the church year as mysterious and ever-present center. Good Friday and the church music of Bach belong together in deepest and inseparable intimacy.

Bach appears before us as a *man of faith.* In this respect his development was determined not only by family tradition but also by his schooling, which was not only theological but bore the imprint of firm confessionalism. Reared in an enviroment of old orthodoxy, he attended the lower classes of the Eisenach Latin School. Here the content of Catechism and Psalter, of (Sunday morning pericopal) Gospels and Epistles was deeply impressed on his mind, for he memorized this material in Latin as well as in German. As a member of the Secunda class in the Ohrdruf *Gymnasium* (classical school) and of the Prima class in the Lüneburg Latin School, he was held to study the classic textbook of orthodoxy, written by Leonhard Hutter. This work introduced him to Lutheran dogmatics and made him intimately acquainted with the teachings of the Lutheran Church. As late as 1773 the *Compendium Hutteri* (1610) was regarded as a bulwark of old Saxon orthodoxy in the schools.

Bach's extensive library included more than eighty theological works. All of these bore marks showing diligent use. One fourth of Bach's library consisted of works by Luther. The other three fourths consisted of books by leaders of Lutheran orthodoxy; their content may be described as being partly dogmatic and polemical and partly practical and "edifying" *(erbaulich)*. Only six volumes were written by mystics and Pietists.

This proportion is significant. It shows both the extent and the direction of Bach's independent study of professional and controversial literature, a study which he undertook after his formal schooling and by means of which he furthered his own education in these fields.

We find that Bach's action is characterized by the fighting mood and spirit of old Lutheranism. It is the same attitude that marked the position he assumed against the Pietistic chief pastor in Mühlhausen; that prompted him to select that minister's orthodox opponent as first sponsor of his first-born son, Friedemann; that caused him to send his children, not to the Reformed public school in Köthen, but to the Lutheran school, and this despite the fact that his sovereign subscribed to the Calvinistic confession; and that impelled him, finally, to use the inside of the cover of the *Notebook* composed for his wife, Anna Magdalena, for a notation to help him remember the titles of three books *(Anti-Kalvinismus, Evangelische Christenschule,* and *Anti-Melancholicus)* by Superintendent Pfeiffer of Lübeck, an old warrior in the battle against doctrinal errors of the Calvinistic, the Pietistic, and the "enlightened" camps.

Just as the pastor-poets of Bach's Weimar cantata libretti were, at the same time, champions of Lutheran orthodoxy, so the mystical element in the music of these Bach cantatas belongs to the master's orthodoxy; that is to say, to a standpoint of faith bound simply and absolutely to the true and genuine confession of the Church.

In making this assertion we must, of course, entirely ignore the contemptuous connotation which the opponents of orthodoxy have often fastened on designations like "orthodox" and "dogmatic." This unfavorable overtone is heard particularly in the literature of Pietism, of rationalistic enlightenment, and also of a new type of Christianity which, in its proud and supercilious conceit, imagines itself to

79

be far above any kind of confessional stand. By means of accusations raised in its literature, this threefold group has launched a vigorous attack against orthodoxy.

Bach, too, had to deal with one or more of these viewpoints. In her comedy *Die Pietisterei im Fischbeinrocke* (1737) the wife of the influential Leipzig poet Gottsched gives the following description: "The very footmen of our day are quarreling about the dark passages of Scripture; and only very recently I heard that a coachman called his horses orthodox, because he could not think of a more abusive word."

The differences between religious confessional writings are caused not only by a variety of religious experiences, moods, and opinions. They go back much farther. They have their roots in other basic differences also. Ethical customs; rites and usages; political, economic, and social views; and, last but not least, development in culture and art — all these areas play an important role in helping to bring about religious differences.

In the field of music, this mighty spiritual and intellectual struggle waged by Lutheran orthodoxy in its battle for pure doctrine and the true confession took various forms. Its principal concern was the secure establishment and development of genuine church music. But the orthodox Lutherans also attacked the "enlightened" group's hostility to music; the separation of church and music, even of school and music, that had taken place in Calvinistic circles in the "church concert" *(Kirchen-Konzert)* and in Pietistic circles in "house and chamber music" *(Haus-*

und Kämmerlein-Musik). Beyond this, the Lutheran group opposed the view which would bring about a cleavage between ecclesiastical and secular music, or between ecclesiastical and secular musical performance in general.

There was nothing surprising about the position that Bach took in the midst of this fray. Ever since the days of his ancestor Veit Bach, fiery zeal for pure doctrine and the true confession had coursed in the veins of the entire generation of Bachs.

THIRD PERIOD: KOETHEN (1717—1723)

At this fateful turning point, however, in the development of German music ca. 1720 Bach's official activity could not reach his declared goal and "final purpose" of a "regulated church music to the glory of God." The reason was that the court of Köthen, where he had been employed since 1717, did not, like the court of Weimar, subscribe to the Lutheran, but to the Calvinistic confession. For that reason Bach did more than to perform his duties as master of chamber music and composer at the royal court. He dedicated himself in increasing measure to instructional activity and to the development of instructional works for clavier. In doing so he worked according to an instructional plan which was not only comprehensive but was also destined to establish a tradition. His plan reminds us of the baroque-universal, vivid instruction found in Comenius' methodical pedagogical text *The Visible World (Orbis pictus)*.

The result was that a third group of compositions (up to 1723) came into being. This group includes

81

the "directions" *(Anleitungen)* of the *Orgelbüchlein,* of the *Klavierbüchlein* for Friedemann Bach and for Anna Magdalena Bach, as well as of the *Well-Tempered Clavier,* of the French and English Suites, and of the *Two- and Thee-Part Inventions,* in addition to a most varied group of concertos and sonatas. In the years of his service at Köthen Bach is prominent as the master teacher.

Bach created compositions possessing merit as patterns for later composers; he encouraged his students to carry on work, like tradesmen, in faithful imitation of the master. After all, this kind of teaching is the real educational goal of music instruction in every era noted for the strength of a tradition.

Already the titles of Bach's instructional compositions — *Anleitungen* (Guides) — point to this goal. So, for example, the title of the *Orgelbüchlein* (1717):

Little Organ Book
in which a Beginner at the Organ
is given Instruction in Developing a Chorale
in many divers ways, and at the same time
in Acquiring Facility in the Study of the Pedal,
since in the Chorales contained therein
the Pedal is treated as Wholly Obbligato
In Praise of the Almighty's Will
And for my Neighbor's Greater Skill [4]

This title indicates the plan of Bach's instruction in the art of playing chorales on the organ. Originally, the entire work was to deal with 164 church

[4] Translation in *The Bach Reader,* p. 75, edited by Hans David and Arthur Mendel. Used by permission.

hymns for Sundays and festival days according to the liturgical order of the church year. Only 56 of the compositions in the project, however, were actually written. The melody of the church hymn is used as *cantus firmus,* usually in the upper voice. It is accompanied by other voices, which not only move contrapuntally but also, with consummate artistry, trace and reflect the spirit of the words in the hymn. A high degree of unity dominates the form of the movement, both as to melody *(Motivik)* and as to rhythm *(Figurik).* Following the tradition of Lutheran church music, these supplementary voices are in the style of instrumental and organ variations based on secular songs and dances.

The title of another work, *Fünfzehn Inventionen und fünfzehn Symphonien,* is similar: Upright Instruction wherein the lovers of the clavier, and especially those desirous of learning, are shown a clear way not alone (1) to learn to play clearly in two voices, but also, after further progress, (2) to deal correctly and well with three obbligato parts; furthermore, at the same time not alone to have good *inventiones* [ideas], but to develop the same well, and above all to arrive at a singing style in playing and at the same time to acquire a strong foretaste of composition. (1723) [5]

From these words it is evident that, for Bach, originality and mastery in performance, improvising, and composing depend less on the gift of a good musical inspiration and the quality of a musical invention *(inventio)* — a theory contradicted by the

[5] Translation in *The Bach Reader,* p. 86.

numerous themes and melodies borrowed by Bach himself — and more on ability to employ creative power successfully in various combinations by means of which the model which has been impressed on the pupil is developed, elaborated, and thoroughly worked out.

The goal envisioned by this pedagogical principle was to be served particularly by the Preludes and Fugues of the *Well-Tempered Clavier* (First Part — 1722). The title announces that this work was intended

For the Use and Profit
of the Musical Youth Desirous of Learning
as well as for
the Pastime of those Already Skilled in this Study.

Bach's course of instruction is described by E. Ludwig Gerber, in the latter's *Lexikon der Tonkünstler.* True enough, the work did not appear until forty years after Bach's death. Yet it provides a fascinating account of the instruction that Gerber's father received from Bach for a period of two years:

> Bach accepted him [my father] with particular kindness because he came from Schwarzburg, and always thereafter called him "Landsmann" [compatriot]. He promised to give him the instruction he desired and asked at once whether he had industriously played fugues. At the first lesson he set his *Inventions* before him. When he had studied these through to Bach's satisfaction, there followed a series of suites, then the *Well-Tempered Clavier.* This latter work Bach played altogether

6 Translation in *The Bach Reader*, p. 85.

84

three times through for him with his unmatchable art, and my father counted these among his happiest hours, when Bach, under the pretext of not feeling in the mood to teach, sat himself at one of his fine instruments and thus turned these hours into minutes. The conclusion of the instruction was thorough bass, for which Bach chose the Albinoni violin solos; and I must admit that I have never heard anything better than the style in which my father executed these basses according to Bach's fashion, particularly in the singing of the voices. This accompaniment was in itself so beautiful that no principal voice could have added to the pleasure it gave me. [7]

Introduction to the art of composing went hand in hand with exercises in instrumental performance and thorough bass. Here, too, Bach always based his instruction on practical activity; everything was centered on example: on having the teacher show how to do something and on having the pupil imitate him. In this connection Ph. Emanuel provides the following account, which provides a brief sketch of his father's course of instruction in the art of composition:

In composition he started his pupils right in with what was practical, and omitted all the dry species of counterpoint that are given in Fux and others.[8] His pupils had to begin their studies by learning pure four-part thorough bass. From this he went to chorales; first he added the basses to

[7] Translation in *The Bach Reader,* pp. 264f.

[8] The reference is to *Gradus ad Parnassum,* by J. J. Fux, published in Latin in 1725. A German version by Mizler appeared in 1742.

them himself, and they had to invent the alto and tenor. Then he taught them to devise the basses themselves. He particularly insisted on the writing out of the thorough bass in (four real) parts *(Aussetzen der Stimmen im Generalbass)*. In teaching fugues, he began with two-part ones, and so on.

The realization of a thorough bass and the introduction to chorales are without doubt the best method of studying composition, as far as harmony is concerned. As for the invention of ideas, he required this from the very beginning, and anyone who had none he advised to stay away from composition altogether. With his children as well as with other pupils he did not begin the study of composition until he had seen work of theirs in which he detected a talent.[9]

In regard to the last sentence we ought to remember, however, that it is the son who speaks here; the father was not familiar with this modern concept of talent, or genius.

Thus, contrary to traditional teaching of vocal counterpoint, which culminated in Fux's *Gradus ad Parnassum* and took its point of departure in settings for two voices, Bach's teaching began with chords in a four-part setting and with the harmonizing of chorales. Continuing, Bach's method led the pupil onward by means of three-part and freely formed four-part settings to the final goal of a harmonically based *Linienkunst* in a strict two-part composition as demanded by Imitation, Canon, and Fugue.

A memorial for this type of instruction has been preserved for us in the *Klavierbüchlein* of 1720.

[9] Translation in *The Bach Reader*, p. 279.

It was prepared by Bach for the instruction of his oldest son, Friedemann, who was ten years old at that time. Designed for instructional purposes, it became the source from which the preludes and fugues in the *Well-Tempered Clavier,* as well as the *Suites* and *Inventions,* were developed.

The significance of works belonging to Bach's Köthen period must be sought first of all in the fact that they offer creative examples *(exempla),* models, and guiding forms of rhythmic, melodic, and harmonic principles. This basic material, offered in Bach's course of instruction, the pupil was to make his own by copying, imitating, and adapting. Bach, of course, possessed extraordinary powers for the production of such materials. He had a rich imagination. He knew how to construct the necessary forms. Moreover, he was able to pattern and develop them according to his own taste and to impart to them the stamp of his own genius. As a result, the examples offered in his course are far above most of the teaching materials used by his contemporaries. What they offered was closely related to school purposes and was utilitarian, but also dry and unimaginative.

These works enable us to obtain a degree of insight into the tradition concerning school and workshop as maintained by Bach and other musicians of his day for their profession. Bach used this pattern material when instructing his own sons and his pupils, even as he himself had studied similar "guide sources" *(Exempelquellen)* when he was taught by his father and his brother.

Another distinction belonging to the patterns Bach placed before his pupils is the living spirit characterizing the manner in which the materials were handed down from one generation to the next. All of them were circulated in transcriptions which Bach's pupils prepared for their own study. In doing so the students subjected the guide material to many a change. They extended or simplified it. In their own way they "improved" the material, especially (until the days of Forkel) in regard to ornamentation.

In these works of the Köthen period, especially in the first part of the *Well-Tempered Clavier,* this tradesmanlike and craftsmanlike master teaching that Bach gave to his pupils lives on undiminished until today. It will continue to live on among music generations yet to come in the most distant future.

We have already heard of Bach's "borrowings." His activity is marked by outstanding examples of this procedure. We find these examples in numerous instances of adaptations, transcriptions, and paraphrases of compositions that he or others had written. All of this work is done with the highest degree of artistry. We might name fugues and themes of Legrenzi, Albinoni, Corelli; concerti by Vivaldi and Duke Johann Ernst of Weimar; compositions by Reinken, Telemann, Marcello; and other models whose origin is unknown.

The spirit in which this practice in imitating musical patterns and guides was carried on is expressed by Mattheson, who says: "Borrowing is entirely permissible, but one must restore the borrowed material with interest; that is, one must so arrange and develop the imitation that it acquires a better and more attractive appearance than the settings from which it has been borrowed." Here, too, we see that what is decisive is the arrangement, development, and execution of the material placed before the pupil. And in the field of church architecture we probably have a closely related type of learning, likewise carried on according to pattern and by imitation of worthy models. The typical church architect of Bach's day gained the mastery of his art by a study of engravings. This is known to have been true of the master of the Dresden council chamber, George Bähr, builder of the Frauenkirche in Dresden. (1726.)

It has rightly been said that in many respects this man, famed as the greatest master of the art of Protestant church building, had a spiritual affinity with Bach, the architect of tonal structure. Just as in Bach's music and in Bach's performance, so also here we have the same spirit and thought filling the wide expanse of this domelike structure, the Frauenkirche, a building known for unheard-of daring in design. It was characteristic of Bähr that in planning this church building he sought to unite clerical with musical elements. The pulpit, as the place of preaching; the font, as the place of baptism; the altar, as the place for liturgy and the Lord's Supper — all these were to be combined with the organ and the organ gallery, the place where music is sounded as part of the divine service. In this way both clerical and musical elements were to arrive at a valid and justified architectonic unity of form as exemplified by the Lutheran-Protestant choir stall. Incidentally, Bähr became personally acquainted with Bach through Gottfried Silbermann, the organ builder and son of an official master carpenter in the Saxon Erzgebirge; Silbermann, in turn, was a friend of Bach.

These musical treasure chests, rich in products of human fantasy, contain musical forms dating back to a Germany of former days. They include the prelude, the fugue, the dance movements of a suite, the invention, and others — forms that have always been characterized by narrowness of range, or format. Already in Bach's day, however, these forms were considered old-fashioned or even hopelessly outdated. Yet these were the very forms that Bach placed before those who came to him to learn. By means of these examples the master saw his pupils grow as craftsmen and artists. Regularly he showed them how he had taken the best of other melodic, rhythmic, and harmonic treasures and had recast them in the fire of his own fantasy. Some of this material had come from German sources, having been produced by town musicians and organists. But the supply included also French harpsichord music, especially the *Charakterstück* of Rameau, as well as the Venetian Concerto of Vivaldi and the Neapolitan Sonata of Scarlatti.

Thus Bach's form of the clavier suite had been modeled according to the pattern set by Froberger. In the English suites the dance forms, although enriched with a polyphonic development of motifs, still appeared in the form of dance music intended for use in actual dances. These suites included the allemande, courante, sarabande, and the gigue; in addition, intermezzi were inserted before the final gigue. In the French suites we find a freer, more delicately sentimental, melodic-homophonic form. To a great extent, the material contained in these suites occurs already in the *Clavierbüchlein* for Anna Magdalena Bach.

Bach's form of the clavier fugue had originated in the same manner. The form he designed was based on a large-scale harmonic ground plan. It was characterized by concertolike arrangement, in which the "development" *(Durchführung)* served as tutti and the intervening material *(Zwischenspiel)* as solo, without even for the duration of one beat setting aside the fundamental elements of obbligato voices and imitation. Other features are the multiform, sharply formulated, "speaking" themes, as well as the prelude, the latter being placed before the fugue but related to the theme of the fugue by having the same mood *(Affekt)* for its fundamental character.[10]

How intimate this last-named relationship, between prelude and the theme of the fugue, can be is observable in the first prelude of the *Well-Tempered Clavier,* a composition which has been greatly admired. Here we have a strict five-part structure (concealed behind the motif of the broken chords) whose upper voice contains the germ of the fugue theme. Such concealed polyphony (not seeming polyphony — *Scheinpolyphonie*) is typical of Bach's highest artistry. It also provides the foun-

---

[10] The word *Affekt* is virtually untranslatable. Helpful discussions of the *Affektenlehre* occur in *Music in Western Civilization,* by Paul Lang, pp. 434 ff.; *Music, History, and Ideas,* by Hugo Leichtentritt, pp. 143 and 149 ff.; *The Bach Reader,* by Hans T. David and Arthur Mendel, pp. 33 f. — O. C. R.

dation for that lineal playing *(Linienspiel)* which captivates both performer and listener in the case of the solo sonatas and the solo suites for a single instrument of melody (violin, flute, violoncello), especially in the virtuoso technique employing the double stop on the violin, a heritage of violin artistry from Old Germany.

In Bach's trio compositions his teaching progresses to a type of setting strictly bound to two voices. It is different from a four-part realization of thorough-bass and chorale playing insofar as the violin, flute, and violoncello sonatas (with fully developed cembalo part) require that the right and left hands of the cembalist carry on two independent lines of melody, which are joined in the trio by the designated instrument of melody. In this arrangement of his trios Bach carried his models, particularly the chamber music of Pachelbel, to the heights of achievement. What he did in this field has exerted an enduring influence on the chamber music of classical and romantic composers. Its influence is noticeable even in our own day among composers who are active in the field of chamber music.

The works of Bach's Köthen period include, finally, the concertos for one and two violins, the orchestral suites *(Französische Ouvertüren),* and the so-called *Brandenburg Concertos.* In these works the master transfers to orchestral and to chamber music the art he had achieved in the field of organ composition. The baroque splendor of their joyousness of tone is heightened. The depth of their tonal range is increased. The pathos suggested by the rhythmical form is intensified.

Bach's orchestra bears all the marks of the tonal fantasy and the style of performance found among the town musicians, and also of the tonal world related to them: the variegated color of tone in the baroque organ. The tone of the choirlike *(chörig)* structure in Bach's musical compositions was fundamentally different in almost every part from the tone provided by the orchestra of the Viennese classicists, the romanticists, or even the neo-romanticists and impressionists. Their hazy line of demarcation between light and dark has often been ascribed to the Bachian orchestra; even today it is wrongly traced back to Bach's standards. The Bach flutes, oboes, bassoons, horns, trumpets, and trombones, as well as his string instruments, are no less basically and no less clearly different from their modern descendants than the Bach cembalo (a plucked instrument) is from the modern piano (a percussion instrument). Throughout, the tone of Bach's instruments is thinner, brighter, more transparent, less strong and massive, but, by way of compensation, more compact and more vigorous, also stronger, than the tone of modern orchestral instruments. The tonal colors of the Bach orchestral instruments are placed, one against the other, in a contrast which is as severe as it is diversified.

As a result, it is possible for the hearer to detect the various elements of strictly polyphonic music. That kind of listening is not possible in the cloudy *(wolkig)* tone of the modern piano (and orchestra) as compared with the fixed tone of the cembalo (and of the baroque organ). Such a contrast in tonal colors achieves a unification in the

93

color of individual instruments in the instrumental choir which is all the greater.

In harmony with his ideal of organ tone (cf. pp. 57 ff.) Bach takes the wind and string choirs of the orchestra of town musicians as solo and accompanying choirs; against these he places the Italian-French string tutti as chief choir. In the dramatic movement of exchange between, on the one hand, the merging full tone of the string choir, swelling and teeming with its own strength, and, on the other hand, the divided tone of the many-colored setting of the concertino we have the culmination of the tonal art of Bach's concerto grosso.

The responsive performer and listener, discovering ever new contrasts, divisions, and mixtures of tone colors of wind and string instruments (which have a value of their own insofar as they are bound strictly to the lineal structure of the work), is surprised and carried away by what he finds. The distinctive power of the tone color that Bach achieves lies in the connection of its individual worth with the bearer of the tone color which it opposes and overcomes. Here we have variety of color appearing as freedom in the midst of dependence. In modern impressionism, on the other hand, we have variety of color that more readily suggests, as its basic causes, lack of control and inability to engage in any kind of resistance.

The *Brandenburg Concertos*, which belong to the concerto grosso type, provide us with the highest order of art as it might be found in courtly society. The compactness of tone and movement in these compositions is resplendent with *joie de vivre* and

94

the optimism of the "fortunate musician" (*glück-seliger Musicus*). Bach wrote these works at the request of Margrave Christian Ludwig of Branden-burg. He dedicated them to the youngest son of the Great Elector, whom the master probably had met during his second stay in Carlsbad in 1720.

After his return from this official tour, which he had undertaken in company with his sovereign, the master was destined to meet with grief that was as unexpected as it was heavy. He was never again to see his wife, Maria Barbara, whom he had left in good health at home in Köthen. Shortly thereafter also his favorite brother died in Ohrdruf. The only brother and sister now living were the brother in Sweden and the unmarried sister in Erfurt.

True enough, Bach was able to provide a new mother for his sons Wilhelm Friedemann, Carl Philipp Emanuel, and Johann Gottfried Bernhard, aged eleven, seven, and six years, respectively. On December 3, 1721, he married the twenty-year-old singer Anna Magdalena Wilcken. She was a descendant of an old generation of Thuringian town musicians. Her father was a member of the guild of court and army trumpeters in Weissenfels.

Like Maria Barbara, Bach's second wife was a musician. For her Bach collected the contents of the now famous *Notenbuch* and had the pages attractively bound with a green cover. The clavier pieces and the songs in this collection mirror some of the tender and delightful scenes that were representative of family life in the home of the master.

On the other hand, Bach was the more depressed by another event which also occurred at this time.

The sovereign who had befriended him married a princess who could best be described as "Amusa."

These heavy calamities and personal trials in Bach's life coincided with that fateful turn in the history of German music which, as we have already noted, took place about 1720. Bach was compelled to recognize that his "final purpose" *(Endzweck)* of providing a "regulated church music to the glory of God" was receding farther and farther into the background. The reason was that the music of his time was declaring itself to be free of obligations that had hitherto bound it, especially in regard to church services. Instead, it was "progressing" more and more toward the freedom promised by the new "enlightenment" and toward a type of musical performance which would be answerable only to itself.

In this serious crisis, as it concerned the development of German music in general and of Bach's creativity in particular, the master's long-range decision to return his art more firmly in its binding obligation to church and to church services and thereby to the tradition of old Lutheran church music assumes most extraordinary significance.

To execute this reorientation and return of his creativity Bach was able to choose one of two posts that were offered him. One proposal, which arrived at the end of 1720, invited him to the Schnitger organ of the Jakobikirche in Hamburg. Five years previously, Neumeister, the poet of Bach's cantata texts, had begun to serve there as chief pastor. Here, under the supervision of 97-year-old Reinken, the probationary performance was to take place. Eight

96

candidates had been invited; Bach was one of them. In the presence of Reinken, Bach indulged in flights of fantasy on the organ of St. Catherine's Church. Astonished by the wealth of beautiful reed stops that the organ possessed, Bach played "for more than two hours." Thereupon, "on the request of those who were present, he improvised very elaborately for almost a half hour, in various forms," on the chorale "By the Waters of Babylon." When he had finished, Reinken expressed his amazement in the words: "I thought that this art had died. I see, however, that it still lives in you." (Necrology.)

Another invitation called the master to Leipzig and asked him to become the successor of Kuhnau (who had died in 1722) as Cantor of St. Thomas School and Church. In his own way, Mattheson provides the following narrative concerning the failure of the proposal that had invited Bach to come to Hamburg:

> I remember, and a whole large congregation will probably also remember, that a few years ago a certain great virtuoso, whose deserts have since brought him a handsome cantorate, presented himself as candidate for the post of organist in a town of no small size, exhibited his playing on the most various and greatest organs, and aroused universal admiration for his ability; but there presented himself at the same time, among other unskilled journeymen, the son of a well-to-do artisan, who was better at preluding with his thalers than with his fingers, and he obtained the post, as may be easily conjectured, despite the fact that almost everyone was

angry about it. This took place just at Christmas
time, and the eloquent chief preacher, who had
not concurred in the Simoniacal deliberations, ex-
pounded in the most splendid fashion the gospel of
the music of the angels at the birth of Christ, in
which connection the recent incident of the rejected
artist gave him quite naturally the opportunity to
reveal his thoughts, and to close his sermon with
something like the following pronouncement: he
was firmly convinced that even if one of the angels
of Bethlehem should come down from Heaven, one
who played divinely and wished to become organist
of St. Jacobi, but had no money, he might just as
well fly away again.[11]

FOURTH PERIOD: LEIPZIG (1723—1745)

Since Hamburg had been lost to him, Bach
elected to become cantor of St. Thomas Church in
Leipzig, although with a somewhat heavy heart. The
post had been rejected by Telemann, Graun, Fasch,
and Graupner, men who were far more famous than
Bach as directors of chamber music at various courts.
When they declined, an architect injected the name
of Bach into the discussion that was being carried
on at a meeting of the Leipzig city council. Graupner,
director of chamber music in Darmstadt, recommended his colleague Bach as a "musician who
was as expert a performer on the organ as he
was experienced in church matters and in chamber
(i. e., concerto) compositions."

On May 5, 1723, the master signed the deed
which documented his appointment as "Cantor of

[11] *The Bach Reader,* pp. 81f.

the School of St. Thomas." His duties were established in fourteen points. Of these, we might note the following:

1. That I shall set the boys a shining example of an honest, retiring manner of life, serve the school industriously, and instruct the boys conscientiously;

2. Bring the music in both the principal churches of this town into good estate, to the best of my ability;

3. Show to the Honorable and Most Wise Council all proper respect and obedience, and protect and further everywhere as best I may its honor and reputation . . .;

5. Not take any boys into the school who have not already laid a foundation in music, or are not at least suited to being instructed therein . . .;

6. So that the churches may not have to be put to unnecessary expense, faithfully instruct the boys not only in vocal but also in instrumental music;

7. In order to preserve good order in the churches, so arrange the music that it shall not last too long, and shall be of such a nature as not to make an operatic impression, but rather incite the listeners to devotion . . .;

10. Faithfully attend to the instruction in the school and whatever else it befits me to do;

11. And if I cannot undertake this myself, arrange that it be done by some other capable person without expense to the Honorable and Most Wise Council or to the school;

12. Not go out of town without the permission of the Honorable Burgomaster currently in office;

13. Always so far as possible walk with the boys at funerals, as is customary;

14. And shall not accept or wish to accept any office in the university without the consent of the Honorable and Learned Council.[12]

Bach was thirty-nine years old when he exchanged the fashionable "Heyducken-Habit" of the court musician for the ancient and venerable cloak of a cantor. He had hoped to conclude his life as master of chamber music in Köthen. Moreover, as he said in a letter to his old Ohrdruf schoolmate, Erdmann: "At first it did not seem at all proper to me that a Capellmeister should become a Cantor." Nevertheless, he says, "I decided to risk it in the name of the Highest." He who had been a *Spielmann* and *Stadtpfeifer* in his childhood years, an organist and *Discantist* in his years of apprenticeship and journeying, *Konzertmeister* and *Hofkapellmeister* had now become the cantor of the principal church and of the principal school in Leipzig, the citadel of Lutheran orthodoxy in Central Germany. Here the *Spielmann Gottes* labored for twenty-seven years until his death.

This fateful decision, to place his daily labors definitely and entirely into the service of the church of the Word and to devote himself to the proclamation of the Word, is one that Bach arrived at in a most notable manner. He was not moved by considerations of what would serve some immediately "practical" purpose, nor by cool, rational deliberations, nor by some willful impulse, nor, for that matter, by purely personal motives of any kind. Instead, he was prompted entirely by reasons of

[12] Ibid., pp. 91 f.

conscience. His attitude represented a victory that he had won by habitual faithfulness on the one hand and by indifference on the other, an attitude giving heed only to the genuineness of the assigned task and of the required confession.

Aside from Leipzig, the only other town to which Bach could have given serious consideration as offering some possibility for the realization of his "final purpose" *(Endzweck)* was Hamburg, known as the North German stronghold of Lutheran orthodoxy and as the "Center of medievalism in the Evangelical Church."

This reversal and "backward" step in the organization of his life and work brought Bach, of course, into the Reformation heritage of the Lutheran school cantorate of St. Thomas Church in Leipzig. It meant that he would follow in the footsteps of Johann Kuhnau, Johann Schelle, Sebastian Knüpfer, Johann Rosenmüller, Tobias Michael, Joh. Hermann Schein, Sethus Calvisius, and others, back into the days of Georg Rhau, who later became the leading printer and publisher of the early Reformation church and school music in Wittenberg.

But to catch the fullest and deepest significance of the move that Bach made we must remember that it took place in the midst of a world whose "enlightenment" had supposedly ushered in a new era. In the light of this circumstance we see that Bach's resolve possessed special meaning for him and for his art and therefore also for the cultivation of German music about 1720. It involved a vital decision, full of the most serious religious implications.

This point was clearly seen by Friedrich Nietzsche. His evaluation, however, was purely negative. In a statement made in 1879, Nietzsche says concerning Bach: "He stands at the threshold of modern European music, but he is always looking back toward the Middle Ages." [13]

The scope of activity for a Lutheran cantor extended beyond the narrow confines of service in church and school. It included faithful work in fostering civic music interests, which were closely intermingled with those of church and school.

Hand in hand with the rise of dilettantism came the decline of the cantorate. As dilettantism and its forms of musical performance for social purposes gained in favor, the profession of cantors and organists lost not only artistic standing but also social and economic worth in the community. With the increasing tendency to make the school autonomous and independent of the church it was inevitable that the figure of the cantor should be moved out of the center of things and be transferred more and more to the periphery of musical culture.

The truth was that even the cantors at St. Thomas were no longer being equipped with the theological and humanistic education that had been characteristic of their own day. The more the old spirit of the Latin school was pushed into the background, and the more frequently a school was highly esteemed because it provided "realistic" or "general education," while a thorough education in music, on the other hand, was regarded more or less as a triviality and

[13] Ibid., p. 374.

a waste of time — so much the more it was bound to happen that the rector and the cantor of a school would engage with increasing intensity in disputes concerning jurisdiction, and that there would be instances of discord.

Bach, too, had much to do because of events of this kind. Musical life at the university and in the academic *Collegia musica* in Leipzig had, in line with the development just indicated, virtually given up any connection with the church. By way of contrast, it had formed increasingly intimate relationships with operatic productions in the city. Already before Bach's day Kuhnau had experienced much grief because of this change. The same experiences were in store for his successor.

With all the means at his command Bach sought to prevent the decay of school and church music as well as to check the curtailment of the cantor's rights. After having officially served Leipzig for seven years he drew up a memorial in which he, as "Director and Cantor at St. Thomas," set forth the reasons that have "necessarily caused the music to decline and to deteriorate." [14] In submitting this document, Bach emphatically cast a sidelong glance at the pampered music conditions prevailing at the royal court of Saxony in Dresden, where August the Strong had permitted large-scale expenditures for his own operatic entertainment and for "an orchestra which is the model for all Europe." Bach continued: "To illustrate this statement with an example one need only go to Dresden and see how the musicians

[14] Ibid., pp. 122 f.

there are paid by His Royal Majesty; it cannot fail, since the musicians are relieved of all concern for their living, free from chagrin, and obliged each to master but a single instrument: it must be something choice and excellent to hear." [15]

The orchestra for the Dresden Opera consisted of approximately twenty stringed instruments and fifteen wind instruments, and the number was increasing every year. Bach, on the other hand, was asking the members of the Leipzig Council to provide only a total of twenty-two instrumentalists (in addition to his sixteen vocalists) for his church orchestra. Of this number, however, and aside from his pupils in the Thomasschule and the university, only "four town pipers *(Stadtpfeifer)*, three professional fiddlers *(Kunstgeiger)*, and one apprentice" [16] were actually at Bach's disposal. Their worth is hinted at by Bach's additional comment: "Modesty forbids me to speak at all truthfully of their qualities and musical knowledge." [17]

Meanwhile, the more difficult it was to preserve the external apparatus needed to foster a "regulated church music to the glory of God" the more energetically the master summoned the last remnants of strength and dignity that could still be found in his declining office as cantor and concentrated them on his real work: the composition of church music. Thus it is that as we now consider a fourth group of works, works of highest maturity, we find the

[15] Ibid., p. 123.
[16] Ibid., p. 121.
[17] Ibid.

foreground occupied by the cantatas written for the festivals and the Sunday church services in the Leipzig churches.

Bach prepared five complete sets of cantatas for the annual cycle of the church year. Of these, 190 have been preserved. About 165 belong to his Leipzig period.

Stylistically, the following group of most important works deserves to be classified under the heading of church cantatas:

the great Latin *Magnificat* (1723), which originally had been provided with chorale inserts for vespers of the First Christmas Day;

the *Christmas, Easter,* and *Ascension Day Oratorios;*

the *B Minor Mass;*

the four *Missae Breves,* more than half of whose individual parts were taken from church or secular cantatas and provided with a Latin text;

also the *Passions According to St. Luke* (1722— of doubtful authenticity), *St. John* (1723), *St. Matthew* (1729), and *St. Mark* (1731—lost). Of these, the last two have a textual and a musical connection with cantatas mourning the death of two persons of high station: the *Passion According to St. Mark* with the funeral ode for Queen Christiane Eberhardine, wife of August the Strong, noted for her loyalty to the Lutheran confessions (1727); the *Passion According to St. Matthew* with the funeral cantata written for the burial of Count Leopold of Köthen (1729).

This fourth group of very mature works includes, in addition, the motets and secular cantatas; also, in the realm of instrumental music, the clavier concertos, the six organ sonatas, the *Concerto Grosso in A Minor* (trio concerto), the fourth part of the *Clavierübung* (with the "Goldberg Variations"), and the second part of the *Well-Tempered Clavier* (1744).

Several years previously Bach had left Weimar to become personally acquainted with Kuhnau in Leipzig. At the time of that visit he had made the following notations for himself concerning the "Order of the Early Church Service in Leipzig on the First Sunday in Advent." On that occasion Bach had presented his cantata *Savior of the Heathen, Come!* in both churches, St. Nicolai and St. Thomas, and had served as organist.

Bach's notations *indicate the high position occupied by music in the liturgical portion of the Communion service* (Messgottesdienst) *in the Lutheran Church of Bach's day,* a service in which the sermon, of course, held the central position. Bach writes:

1. "Preluding." [18] This was the place for a larger, freely formed organ work — a fantasia, toccata, or prelude.

2. "Motetta." In place of the Introit of the old Mass, the opening of the church service brought a Latin or German motet in somewhat ancient style

[18] From Nos. 1 to 14, the sections in quotation marks at the beginning of each numerical division are rendered in translation in *The Bach Reader,* p. 70.

from the collection of motets of the seventeenth century. Bach himself no longer wrote motets except for special occasions, as, for example, in the case of a death. We have an illustration in his great five-part burial motet *Jesu, meine Freude*.[19] This work consists of eleven sections (variations), alternately based on the six chorale stanzas and on five Bible verses (from Romans 8). The structure of the composition makes it a work of art. The chorale fugue, "Ihr aber seid nicht fleischlich, sondern geistlich" (But ye are not in the flesh, but in the Spirit — Rom. 8:9), serves as the center. The remainder of the material, consisting of five sections each, is grouped about it, coming either before or after. The entire composition is placed in a framework in which the first and the last stanzas of the chorale, each set in simple, four-part harmony, form the beginning and the end. — In those days motets were used to open not only the early service on Sunday mornings (matins) but also the vesper service. This is the reason why today the latter is still known as "motet" *(Motette),* not only in St. Thomas Church but also elsewhere.

3. "Preluding on the Kyrie, which is performed throughout." Using the motet form, the school choir sang the Kyrie eleison of the old Mass completely in its three parts (Kyrie, Christe, Kyrie eleison), as we have them in Bach's *Missa Brevis,* Nos. 1—4. Often these sections were given a vernacular turn;

19 1723. — *Jesus, Priceless Treasure.* The chorale may be found in *The Lutheran Hymnal,* No. 347.

e. g.: "Kyrie, God Father Eternal," "Christe, Our Only Hope," "Kyrie, God Holy Ghost."[20]

4. "Intoning before the altar." The minister chanted the first line of the "Gloria in excelsis Deo."

5. "Reading of the Epistle." Standing at the altar, the minister read the Epistle appointed for that Sunday.

6. "Singing of the Litany."

7. "Preluding on the Chorale." The organist played a chorale prelude on the hymn which was sung by the congregation and which had come to take the place of the Gradual of the old Mass. This was the principal hymn (Hauptlied) of the Sunday. — The designation "chorale prelude" takes us back in history to the introduction of organ accompaniment for congregational singing, an innovation which occurred about the middle of the seventeenth century. The term must not be confused with "organ chorale" (Orgelchoral). The latter term implies that the organist would be required to take the chorale from beginning to end (per omnes versus) and that he would be expected to provide as many variations on the organ as there were stanzas in the hymn. The term "chorale prelude," on the other hand, indicates that only the first member in this proposed series of variations would be played on the organ; the members (stanzas) that followed were to be sung by the congregation together with organ accompaniment.

8. "Reading of the Gospel."

[20] No. 6 in *The Lutheran Hymnal.*

108

9. "Preluding on the principal composition (cantata)." By means of a free improvisation, the organist introduces the presentation of the cantata scheduled to be heard on that Sunday. The cantata was the principal music *(Hauptmusik)* of the day. It was heard either before or, if divided, before and after the sermon. Together with the sermon, the cantata shared the responsibility of making the congregation receptive for the proclamation of the Gospel and of collaborating in expounding the Biblical message and making it vivid. In other words, the cantata, like all musical performance in church, singing as well as playing, was to find its fulfillment in preparing the way for the preacher and the sermon, in opening the hearts of congregation members for the entrance of the Word of God, and thus making the assembled people a "hearing congregation." "Solae aures sunt organa Christiani hominis," Luther once said in deprecating the visible elements of a church service: "Hearing is the only tool of a Christian person." Thus Bach's church cantata, too, is a kind of "shortened sermon" (Neumeister). Even in its textual form the cantata appears before us in a pattern resembling the structure of the sermon, whose framework places the component elements *(propositio, tractatio,* and *applicatio)* between the *exordium* (introduction) and *conclusio.* As a rule, the cantata begins with an opening chorus, which corresponds to the introductory prayer, text, and theme of the sermon. This opening chorus has been developed on the basis of the chief or "sermon hymn" *(Haupt- oder Predigtlied)* of the particular Sunday. The final part of the cantata again agrees in spirit

109

with the sermon, this time with the concluding prayer of the sermon. This closing section consists of a stanza of a church hymn set in simple, four-part harmony. It was sung and played by all singers and performers who had had a part in the cantata. The middle portion of the sermon sustained a certain mood *(Affekt)* by its treatment *(tractatio)* and application *(applicatio)* of the text. The middle section of the sermon found a corresponding musical expression in the cantata. In the dramatic movement achieved by the secco recitatives and the arias, duets, and chorus numbers (the last three being used particularly to continue the mood of the sermon), the text consisted mostly of free recastings, or paraphrases, of the stanzas of the principal hymn *(Hauptlied)*. — The arias and duets of Bach's cantatas follow the threefold arrangement of the Neapolitan da capo aria, or, respectively, the Vivaldi concerto type. The principal theme is stated twice, at the beginning and at the end of the aria; between these two sections, in the middle, there is another theme; thus the aria consists of three sequential divisions. The first statement of the principal theme is preceded by a ritornello (symphonic introduction), announcing this theme. The middle portion, bringing the second theme, is somewhat shorter than the first and third sections. When the middle section has been completed, the principal theme returns (da capo) to constitute the third part of the aria.

10. "Singing of the Creed." Immediately after the cantata, or after its first part, the congregation

sang Luther's German translation of the Nicene Creed, "We all believe in one true God." [21]

11. "The Sermon." Central point and climax of the divine service.

12. "After the Sermon, as usual, singing of several stanzas of a hymn." When the sermon had been ended, the congregation sang the hymn "Our Father, Thou in heaven above." [22] Thereupon the congregation sang a hymn to introduce the celebration of the Lord's Supper, which followed immediately. The hymn was either "To Jordan came our Lord, the Christ," [23] or the hymn of repentance, "From depths of woe I cry to Thee." [24]

13. "Words of Institution (of the Sacrament)." At the altar, the minister read the New Testament account of the Lord's institution of the Sacrament of the Altar.

14. "Preluding on the composition (probably the second part of the cantata). After the same, alternate preluding and singing of chorales until the end of the Communion, et sic porro." During the Communion it was customary to present the second portion of the cantata; or, church hymns were sung or performed alternately by the congregation or

21 The original melody, sung in Bach's day, is listed as the "Second Tune" for No. 251 in *The Lutheran Hymnal*. Fortunately, it is being reintroduced in American congregations.

22 No. 458 in *The Lutheran Hymnal*.

23 No. 401 in an earlier hymnbook published by Concordia Publishing House (St. Louis, Mo.), *Evangelical Lutheran Hymn-Book*.

24 No. 329 in *The Lutheran Hymnal*.

choir, or on the organ. After the thanksgiving collect and the benediction an organ postlude of larger proportions ended the Communion service *(Messgottesdienst)*.

In this strictly joined liturgical order of the Lutheran Mass, in which the preaching service and the celebration of Communion had not yet been separated, the "regulated church music" of Bach finds its liturgical place. By virtue of the Biblical text of the sermon the pertinent principal hymn, or sermon hymn *(Predigtlied)*, and its melody acquired central significance, in an ever greater degree, as *cantus firmus* in the cantatas of Bach.

The emphasis that Bach gave to the chorale was not a "natural" development, in harmony with the spirit of his day; rather, it was the reverse. Even in the church cantatas which had been written by Bach's predecessor, Kuhnau, and which also had already adopted the da capo aria and the secco recitative, the chorale had receded almost entirely into the background. It was Bach who first rewon for the church cantata not only the Bible text but also the old Luther hymns. To make room for these, Bach relegated the emotionalized songs of devotion and sentiment, which bore the stamp and imprint of Buxtehude, to a less prominent position.

As we examine the tradition preserved among the cantors of St. Thomas, we find that Bach's chorale cantatas were not linked to Kuhnau but to Johann Schelle and the seventeenth century. After 1735 Bach even went to the extent of composing a complete set of *chorale cantatas* for a full year. Most prominent among these are the great cantatas based

112

on Luther's hymns: "All praise to Thee, eternal God," "Now praise we Christ, the Holy One," "In peace and joy I now depart," "To Jordan came our Lord, the Christ," "From depths of woe I cry to Thee," "Lord, keep us steadfast in Thy Word." [25]

In doing the necessary work of paraphrasing the texts of Bible passages and church hymns and making these ready for use as texts in the arias and recitatives of cantatas, the master was assisted by Henrici (Picander), the *Ober-Post-Commissarius* of Leipzig.[26]

Already in the composition of the cantata *Christ lag in Todesbanden* (1724), Bach had written a chorale cantata "per omnes versus." All the seven sections of this cantata are based on the seven stanzas of Luther's Easter hymn; each stanza appears in the form of a chorale variation.

In his later chorale cantatas Bach uses the appointed sermon hymn *(Predigtchoral)* as *cantus firmus* in an introductory section of broad design. The first and last stanzas appear in their original form; moreover, Bach always uses the original melody of the hymn. In other sections of the cantata the chorale melody also takes possession of elements which might normally be considered foreign to the chorale, like the aria and the recitative. The chorale penetrates these forms with the great, basic powers of its melody, as we see in chorale arias, chorale

[25] Respectively, Nos. 80, 104, 137, 401, 329, and 261. All numbers, except No. 401, refer to *The Lutheran Hymnal;* No. 401 is in the *Evangelical Lutheran Hymn-Book.*

[26] The title corresponds to that of postmaster in an American city.

113

choruses, and chorale sinfonias. Or the chorale appears in the background; the symbolic power of its *cantus firmus,* however, is not reduced because of this position.

We have an illustration of the latter device in the Reformation Cantata *Ein' feste Burg ist unser Gott* (1730). Here the chorale appears without words in oboes, trumpets, and continuo. The arrangement provides an excellent picture of the church and portrays her as she bears testimony in a heroic confession. The enlargement of the chorale-*cantus firmus* foundation in the bass seems to point to the superhuman defensive power and security of the "Mighty Fortress." In the same spirit, the canon of the twofold presentation of the chorale by means of trumpet and continuo seems to say that the power and severity of church doctrine and of obedience in faith embrace heaven and earth.

Other works that Bach composed are related to the chorale cantatas, not only because of the style that he employed in these works but also because of the fact that they were designed to be used in the church service. We think, of course, of the chorale motets; not only of *Jesu, meine Freude,* but above all of *O Jesu Christ, meins Lebens Licht* (1740), which was a funeral motet, like *Jesu, meine Freude,* with obbligato accompaniment provided by wind instruments. But there are others in this group; not only the cantata masses and the cantata oratorios but also the Passions. All of these belong in the general classification of chorale cantatas.

The writing of musical scores for Passions had received lively support particularly in Hamburg in connection with opera that was flourishing there. In composing his *St. John Passion* Bach followed the style of the Passion oratorio currently prevailing in Hamburg. Georg Philipp Telemann has given us a vivid description of that style. For his *St. Matthew Passion*, based on a text by the Hamburg poet Brockes (used also by Händel), Telemann provided the following significant title: "The painful but also refreshing memory of the suffering and death of Jesus. Composed for the edification of pious souls according to the text of the holy Evangelist Matthew and provided here and there with arias and chorales. Presented during Passiontide in the churches of Hamburg in 1722 and set to music by G. Ph. Telemann." Bach also took over Brockes' allegorical figures, such as "the Christian Church," "the soul of the believer," and other poetic conceptions inserted in the Biblical text of the Gospel.

Just as "church music" *(Kirchenmusik)* in the style of the motet was crowded out by the cantata and its concert-style of music, so the "Passion-music" and its style of liturgical chant were replaced by the concerto type of Passion-oratorio with its arias and recitatives, its paraphrases of the texts of church hymns and the melodies of chorales.

In adopting the newer forms Telemann sought to meet the violent opposition of the orthodox clergy in Hamburg by referring specifically to Klopstock and Neumeister. Bach, on the other hand, ranged himself with those who opposed any relaxing of the liturgical obligation of the Passion music; he would not have its function in the church service

115

weakened by emotionalized, meditative texts and by the subjectivism of hymns of "edification" *(Erbauungslieder)*. Just as Bach had brought the composition of cantatas back to the chorale cantata as the proper basis, so he bound the composition of Passions to the liturgy as the original source of power.

To achieve his goal, Bach regained for the evangelist of the Passion the pure word of the Bible; for the congregation of believers he recaptured the universal and confessional hymn of the Lutheran Church. In his neat and exact copy of the *St. Matthew Passion* the master used a carefully considered and significant device: he used red ink only for the Biblical words of the text assigned to the evangelist and for the chorale *cantus firmus* (in the opening chorale fantasia for double chorus).

The thoughtful planning reflected in the basic outline of Bach's *St. Matthew Passion* deserves our careful study. The grouping of individual passages according to key and tonal association reveals a drama of basic movement pervading the whole of its Passion story which affords a vista into eternal life beyond all music that deals with death and the grave, with dying and the evening of life.

In a significant allegory, the congregation of believers joins in the prayers and in the confession of the facts of salvation contained in the Passion of Christ. Thus the congregation is drawn into the redeeming death of the Lord. Moreover, by means of the chorales woven in here and there the congregation is brought into a living relationship with the individual places on Christ's pathway of suffering and is exhorted to engage in a testimony of the Gospel.

Thus in the second part of the *Passion* the recitative of the evangelist, "And they spit upon Him, and took the reed, and smote Him on the head," is answered with the chorale, "O sacred Head, now wounded, with grief and shame weighed down." Again, the recitative, "Jesus, when He had cried again with a loud voice, yielded up the ghost," is answered with the chorale, "When mine hour comes for parting, Lord, part not Thou from me." Similar relationships are responsible for the manner in which the remaining individual passages are bound to their particular position in the entire scheme of the dramatic progress.

This powerful method of pointing and directing everything to the hearer achieves a wonderful effect. The listener is drawn into the redemptive suffering and death of Christ. Thereby he is led into all the depth of that Christian piety which is bound to the Cross. Moreover, by means of this intimate relationship between narration and audience we are enabled to see that the Biblical events, bound by time, possess a content which is over and above all time. We see the value of the past for the present. We experience in the Passion history a living feeling of its present worth.

Who can say what help the *St. Matthew Passion* has given, both extensively and intensively, to suffering humanity? Who will venture to describe with what effect particularly the melodies of the chorales, and among them especially the chorale "When mine

117

hour comes for parting" ("Wenn ich einmal soll scheiden"), have, in Bach's setting, helped men bear their grief and have dispensed the comfort of the Gospel? The number of instances goes beyond the range of human thought.

In his memoirs, Hector Berlioz gives the following account concerning the presentation of the *St. Matthew Passion* in Berlin in 1843:

> When a person comes from Paris and is familiar with our musical customs, he must first be a personal witness of the attentiveness, the respect, and the piety with which the German public listens to a composition of that kind, if he is to believe that such audiences exist. It is really true: everyone follows the words of the textbook with his eyes; there is not a single movement in the auditorium, not a murmur, whether of agreement or of criticism, nor an indication of approval. One is in church and hears the Gospel sung. He silently attends, not a concert, but a church service. And this is the only way in which to hear this music. One adores Bach, one believes in him, without for a moment yielding to the thought that his divinity could ever be doubted. We are not permitted even to mention such heresy. A heretic would be regarded as an abomination. Bach is Bach, even as God is God.[27]

In a letter to his student friend Erwin Rhode on April 30, 1870, Friedrich Nietzsche writes: "During the current week I heard the *St. Matthew Passion* of the divine Bach three times, always with the same feeling of immeasurable wonderment. Who-

[27] Persons of informed judgment will know what to do with these extravagant statements. — O. C. R.

ever has completely forgotten *(verlernt)* what Christianity is will really hear it here as a Gospel." [28]

When the *St. Matthew Passion* was first presented in the Thomaskirche of Leipzig, on Good Friday, 1729, it was widely considered too "theatrical." So, for example, a pious lady of noble birth is said to have exclaimed: "God save us, my children! It's just as if one were at an opera comedy." [29] Nor did Bach follow this course of dramatic composition any farther. Instead, he composed the *B Minor Mass* for the Dresden court, which, ever since August the Strong had changed his religion (1697), had become Catholic.

The *B Minor Mass*, like the other works discussed above, is written in the form of a gigantic cycle of cantatas. According to the score written in Bach's own hand, the composition falls into a group of four works: the real Missa (or, according to Lutheran terminology, the Kyrie-Gloria group), the Nicene Creed (the Credo group), the Sanctus, and the Osanna-group.

In the *B Minor Mass* Bach uses a unique device to assert the truth that the basic treasures of the Christian religion are the common possession of all members of the universal Christian Church. In constructing the five-part opening and concluding

[28] A scholarly and stimulating discussion of this phase of Nietzsche's life was provided in America by Dr. Heinz Bluhm. His valuable article, "Das Lutherbild des jungen Nietzsche," was published in Volume LVIII (March, 1943) of the *Publications of the Modern Language Association*, pp. 264—288. — O. C. R.

[29] Translation in *The Bach Reader*, p. 229.

chorus of the Credo group, he based it on the Gregorian melodies of the ancient church, "Credo in unum Deum" and "Confiteor unum baptisma," and used these as powerful *cantus firmi*.

Bach's *B Minor Mass* is a brilliant companion piece for Händel's coronation anthem for George II of England. Bach's work was written to express the Leipzig citizens' oath of fealty for Bach's sovereign, the Elector August II, son and successor of August the Strong (1733).

Only the Kyrie-Gloria group was presented for the occasion of the homage. The other three groups were most probably written by Bach because he expected to be commissioned to prepare a coronation mass for the crowning of the Elector in Cracow as King of Poland. True enough, these three portions were not to be publicly performed on this occasion, but they were to acquire for him a title that he had requested, "Hof-Compositeur der Kurfürstlich Sächsischen Hof-Capelle" in Dresden. From the electoral court of Saxony in Weissenfels (occupied by the incumbent by the right of a younger son) Bach had already in 1723 received a title he had asked for, "Kapellmeister von Haus aus."

In comparison with Bach's church cantatas, which were intended for the church service, his secular cantatas play only a secondary role, regardless of how significant some of the compositions are that belong to this group. The best-known Leipzig compositions in this category are the so-called Peasant and Coffee Cantatas, which are in the nature of "family cantatas." The former of the two, beginning with the words, "Mer han e neue Oberkeet" (1742—

120

"We have a new government"), was intended for use in paying homage to the Chamberlain of Dieskau at Klein-Zschocher (near Leipzig).

An interesting contrast with these lesser compositions is provided by a pretentious work that appeared in Leipzig in the years extending from 1726 to 1730. It was the first edition of Opus 1, entitled *Clavierübung*.

Keyboard Practice
consisting of
Preludes, Allemandes, Courantes, Sarabandes, Gigues, Minuets, and other Gallanteries
Composed for Music Lovers, to Refresh their Spirits
(*Gemuets-Ergoetzung*)
by
Johann Sebastian Bach
Actual *Capellmeister* to His Highness
the Prince of Anhalt-Köthen
and
Directore Chori Musici Lipsiensis [30]

This is one of the few works of Bach that were printed during the lifetime of the master. In these *partitas* Bach's free and individual powers of invention bring the cycle of the clavier suite and its sequence of clearly defined dance forms into the immediate proximity of the classic-romantic *Charakter- und Stimmungsstücke*, as, e. g., the sarabande. Following Domenico Scarlatti's clavier technique, Bach leads these movements in the direction of the slow movement of the sonata.

[30] *The Bach Reader*, p. 105.

The title of the second part of the *Clavierübung* (1735) announces that the work consists of "a concerto after the Italian taste and an overture after the French manner for a harpsichord with two manuals." [31] The fourth part (1742), the title states, consists of "an aria with divers variations for the harpsichord with two manuals." [32]

These two works, particularly the *Italian Concerto,* the *Suite in B Minor* (also called *Overture in the French Manner),* and the *Goldberg Variations* constitute incomparably high peaks in the realm of creativity that produces free forms and yet is also strictly bound to form. In these works Bach has scaled the summits in the art of composing concertos, suites, and ostinato variations.

These works were no longer circulated in the manner that Bach formerly had been obliged to use. Hitherto he had submitted the instructional material in manuscript form as a guide for the individual pupil or apprentice, who was then held to copy them for himself. This had been the procedure even in the case of the second part of the *Well-Tempered Clavier,* which was completed in 1744. Instead, these works were circulated in printed form among the members of the growing circle of courtly, noble, and middle-class "amateurs and connoisseurs" ("Liebhaber und Kenner") for the purpose of "refreshing their spirits."

The third part of the *Clavierübung* appeared in 1739. It consisted of a collection of organ com-

[31] *The Bach Reader,* p. 133.

[32] Ibid., p. 171.

positions. The title reads: *Third Part of the Keyboard Practice, Consisting of Various Preludes on the Catechism and Other Hymns for the Organ. For Music Lovers and Especially for Connoisseurs of Such Work.*[33] The contents of this work, a kind of second part of the *Orgelbüchlein,* prove that the keyboard instruments of Bach's day still formed a musical community.

In the production of this work the Thomas cantor, still pursuing his goal of a "regulated church music," created a cycle for organ playing in the church service. Since this "Organ Mass" *(Orgelmesse)* was to be patterned according to the Lutheran Communion service *(Messgottesdienst),* Bach opens it with a concertante prelude in E flat "pro Organo pleno." It is ended with the "Trinity" Fugue. There now follow (always in two settings — one wrought with great artistry, the other relatively simple in form) patterns for organ compositions used in the preaching service: the German Kyrie, Christe, Kyrie, and Gloria ("Allein Gott in der Höh' sei Ehr'" — "All glory be to God on high," *The Lutheran Hymnal,* No. 237); the hymn on the Ten Commandments ("That man a godly life might live," *The Lutheran Hymnal,* No. 287); the German Credo, "We all believe in one true God" *(The Lutheran Hymnal,* No. 251); and the Lord's Prayer hymn ("Our Father, Thou in heaven above" — *The Lutheran Hymnal,* No. 458); also the settings of organ music used during the Communion service: the Baptismal hymn, "To Jordan came our Lord, the Christ"; the hymn of repent-

[33] Ibid., p. 164.

ance, "From depths of woe I cry to Thee" (*The Lutheran Hymnal,* No. 329), and the Communion hymn, "Jesus Christ, our blessed Savior, turned away God's wrath forever" (*The Lutheran Hymnal,* No. 311).

In addition to these we have, as permanent models for organ music during the celebration of Communion, *the four Duets*. They are cast in the form of large-scale two-part inventions. They correspond in length to the great amount of time needed for the distribution of the Lord's Supper to the large number of St. Thomaskirche members who appeared as guests at the Lord's Table.

During Bach's last two decades the master withdrew more and more from public activity. At the same time, however, he made use of his self-imposed solitude in ceaseless activity, and reaped an abundant harvest.

Externally, these years are interrupted only by several journeys to the nearby courts of Dresden and Potsdam. Here the Thomas cantor observed the musical life carried on under August the Strong and August II in Dresden and under Frederick the Great in Berlin. His visits were not limited to passive observation but were marked also by active and critical participation.

In Dresden Bach made many a visit, especially in the circle of his music-loving patrons, the Imperial Counts von Flemming, von Keyserlingk, and von Sporck. The chamber music group of the electoral court of Saxony, long known for its excellence, was the possessor of a very important musical tradition, also in regard to performance on the violin and the lute. Bach had written his sonatas and suites specifically for the skillful court violinist Joh. Georg Pisendel. Silvius Leopold Weiss, on the other hand, the court lutenist, with whom Bach had engaged in a contest for cembalo and lute, had stimulated Bach to write his compositions for the lute.

Together with his son Friedemann, Bach had visited the sumptuous court theater and had attended the presentation of Joh. Adolf Hasse's opera *Cleofide* (1731). At this occasion he had performed publicly on the Silbermann organ of the Sophienkirche, "in the presence of all the musicians and virtuosi of the court." Later, when Friedemann Bach was given an organ post, he was assigned to this same organ. Five years later, in connection with his solemn acceptance of another title, that of court composer, Bach dedicated the new Silbermann organ in the Frauenkirche of Dresden. On that occasion he played "for two hours, arousing the intense admiration" of his hearers. The group of listeners included his patron of the nobility, the Imperial Count von Keyserlingk, as well as other members of the circle of noblemen at the electoral court of Saxony. They were friends of music and admirers of Bach's artistry.

"Friedemann," the master was accustomed to say with reference to the art prevailing at the Dresden court, "shall we go again and hear the lovely little ditties *(Liederchen,* songlets) in Dresden?" In using the term Bach probably had reference also to the opera arias of his friend Hasse. The master is said to have spoken in a similarly disparaging vein in regard to the cultivation of music at the court of Potsdam, where Philipp Emanuel Bach had been appointed cembalist *(Kammer-Cembalist)* ever since Frederick the Great had ascended the throne. " 's ist Berliner Blau, das verschiesst." ('Tis Prussian Blue; it will prove worthless.)

Incidentally, musical activities at the court of Potsdam were determined by the Graun Brothers and Joh. Joachim Quantz, the famous flute instructor of Frederick the Great. After the death of August the Strong (1733) the Electorate of Saxony, the little patriarchal church-state of Lutheranism, was gradually superseded, also in the field of music, by Brandenburg, a secular state of increasing power.

Forkel provides an impressive narrative concerning the memorable event in Potsdam when the Thomas cantor personally met Frederick the Great (1747), the monarch who could be interested in German art only by means of music. Forkel has given us the following oral account of Friedemann Bach:

> At this time the King used to have every evening a private concert, in which he himself generally performed some concertos on the flute. One evening, just as he was getting his flute ready and his musicians were assembled, an officer brought him the written list of the strangers who had arrived. With his flute in his hand, he ran over the list, but immediately turned to the assembled musicians and said, with a kind of agitation: "Gentlemen, old Bach is come." The flute was now laid aside; and old Bach, who had alighted at his son's lodgings, was immediately summoned to the Palace. . . . At that time it was the fashion to make rather prolix compliments. The first appearance of J. S. Bach before so

great a king, who did not even give him time to change his traveling dress for a black cantor's gown, must necessarily be attended with many apologies. . . .

But what is more important than this is that the King gave up his concert for this evening and invited Bach, then already called the Old Bach, to try his fortepianos, made by Silbermann, which stood in several rooms of the Palace. The musicians went with him from room to room, and Bach was invited everywhere to try them and to play unpremeditated compositions. After he had gone on for some time, he asked the King to give him a subject for a fugue in order to execute it immediately without any preparation. The King admired the learned manner in which his subject was thus executed extempore; and, probably to see how far such art could be carried, expressed a wish to hear also a fugue with six obbligato parts. But as not every subject is fit for such full harmony, Bach chose one himself and immediately executed it to the astonishment of all present in the same magnificent and learned manner as he had done that of the King. His Majesty desired also to hear his performance on the organ. The next day, therefore, Bach was taken to all the organs in Potsdam as he had before been to Silbermann's fortepianos. After his return to Leipzig, he composed the subject which he had received from the King in three and six parts, added several intricate pieces in strict canon on the subject, had it engraved, under the title of *Musicalisches Opfer (Musical Offering)*, and dedicated it to the inventor.

This was Bach's last journey.[84]

[84] *The Bach Reader*, pp. 305 f.

FIFTH PERIOD: LEIPZIG (1745—1750)

Bach wrote his last church cantata in 1744. With the composition of this work he had reached his goal. He now returned to that realm in which he had begun — the art of composing works for keyboard instruments. All the resources he had acquired in his ascent to the heights of mastery were now concentrated on an art producing canons and fugues of strictest form.

The fifth and last group of works (1745 to 1750) includes the following compositions:

The canonic variations on *Vom Himmel hoch, da komm ich her* (1746),[35]
The *Musical Offering* (1747),
Two separate canons,
The last organ chorales,
The *Art of the Fugue (Kunst der Fuge).*

All of these are works for clavier. The meaning of the term is the one that was current in those days: it referred to a keyboard instrument that was to be played "manualiter" and "pedaliter," regardless of whether the instrument might be an organ, a clavicembalo, or a clavichord.

These unique works, composed by Bach in his advanced years, bring the German art of keyboard performance to the limit of artistic possibilities. The influence of Bach's decision to return to former standards in regard to vocal music and to bind his vocal compositions once again to the tradition found

[35] "From heaven above to earth I come." — The chorale may be found as No. 85 in *The Lutheran Hymanl.*

in old Lutheran church music is operative also here, in the realm of keyboard music.

Bach's variations on Luther's Christmas hymn "Vom Himmel hoch, da komm ich her" (From Heaven above to earth I come) are cast in a decidedly antique mold. They are reminiscent of the early days of German organ music, of artists in performance like Samuel Scheidt. In the final analysis, the work goes far beyond even those days and reaches back to the late medieval origin of the whole art of chorale treatment and exploitation: the Gothic "organum."

In this great canon Bach intensifies and enriches the "organal" tension between a chorale-*cantus firmus* on the one hand, which moves onward in its course of superhuman symmetry according to the eternal law of the spheres, and, on the other hand, a superstructure in which movement is the result of a wealth of human materials and an abundance of human fantasy. The two contrapuntal voices are bound to one another in the form of a strict canon. In the end the chorale, too, is drawn into this realm of binding law.

By means of Bach's artistry this work becomes an exalted symbol *(Sinnbild)* of Christian existence. It portrays the tension between the mundane and the supramundane world, between time and eternity.

Keeping in mind the allegorical value of the symbol, we shall find the canonic variations to be richly suggestive. The Luther chorale, serving here both as foundation and as scaffold of the musical structure, may be said to point to the unshakable edifice of the church. The *cantus firmus* style says: the confessing, testifying life of the Christian must be bound to dogma. The canonic form of the contrapuntal voices speaks of the obedience which a Christian person renders in his life of faith, and of his freedom in the midst of dependence and subordination. The compact three-part setting pictures the all-pervading government and control exercised by the divine Trinity. Finally, the universal character of the baroque organ tone suggests the divine order of creation and the harmony of the universe.

But the symbolical power of this work of art carries us to even greater heights. We notice that even the smallest and subtlest motion, beginning with the first tone and beat and continuing to the last, is carefully arranged and subordinated with reference to the structural plan and outline of the whole work. Moreover, although the manifold variety of form and inventiveness bears the full imprint of richly imaginative fantasy, everything is penetrated by an inner force of law whose mode of operation is as concise as it is compelling.

As a result of all these factors this great work of art becomes more than a symbol of human existence. By combining profound thought with contrapuntal skill it grows upward into an exalted picture of the creative power of God. It becomes "a mirror of the divine order and a foretaste of the heavenly harmony" *(ein Spiegel göttlicher Ordnung und ein Vorgeschmack der himmlischen Harmonie).*

The reason why the remaining later works of the master are marked by the same vitality as that which flows through the canonic variations is that the same symbolic power of Christian art in its German, Lutheran form operates upon them and in them as a living force. Yet these works experienced a strange fate. After the master's death they were no longer understood and were subsequently forgotten.

This group includes first of all the Schübler Chorales, named after the publisher, Schübler, who issued them in Zella near Suhl. There were also eighteen other chorales "of various kinds, to be played on an organ with two claviers (manuals) and pedal."

In these works, the tension created by the play of contrapuntal voices which are held to careful observance of the design of motifs is relaxed. Instead, Bach employs songlike, transparent, and periodically recurring forms. These devices, however, serve only to deepen and to intensify the symbolic contrast between temporal and eternal, between natural and supernatural values.

When the St. Thomas cantor visited Frederick the Great in Potsdam, the royal monarch played the theme of a fugue on a clavier and then asked Bach to develop it. "I noticed very soon, however," the master later wrote in a letter to the King, "that for lack of necessary preparation, the execution of the task did not fare so well as such an excellent theme demanded. I resolved therefore and promptly pledged myself to work out this right Royal theme more fully and then to make it known to the world. This resolve has now been carried out as well as possible, and it has none other than this irreproachable intent, to glorify, if only in a small point, the fame of a Monarch whose greatness and power, as all the sciences of war and peace, so especially in music, everyone must admire and revere." [36]

These words, expressing deep emotion, accompanied the work that Bach sent to the King on July 7, 1747. Entitled *Musical Offering*, it was meant to be a kind of musical homage to the royal hero. It consisted of a fugue and several canons based on the fugal theme that the King had submitted, and also of a sonata for flute, violin, and clavier.

The *Art of the Fugue* (1749) may well be called the musical testament of Bach. It consists of a cycle of twenty fugues and canons. The work was to culminate in a final, mirror-like, retrogressive, inverted giant fugue. This last part remained uncompleted. Bach's handwriting ends at the point where the master, now turned blind, intended, as it were, to add his mark, B-A-C-H, to the structure and to insert it as the sign of a stonecutter.

Although Bach's eyes and hands were paralyzed, the urge and also the power to create continued on. Dictating to his son-in-law, Altnikol, Bach provided a final form for two organ chorales: one based on Luther's Easter and Communion hymn, "Jesus Christus, unser Heiland, der den Tod überwand," the other based on Luther's Pentecost hymn, "Komm, Gott Schöpfer, Heiliger Geist." [37] Also, during the early part of July 1750 he dictated the beginning

[36] *The Bach Reader,* p. 179.
[37] No. 233 in *The Lutheran Hymnal.*

of an organ chorale based on Paul Eber's hymn "Wenn wir in höchsten Nöten sein." [38] Because death was near, Bach provided this organ chorale with the text of a hymn regularly sung to this melody, and whose words, in the first and last stanzas, Bach was even then praying:

> Vor deinen Thron tret' ich hiemit,
> O Gott, und dich demütig bitt',
> Wend dein genädig Angesicht
> Von mir blutarmen Sünder nicht.
>
> Ein selig Ende mir bescher,
> Am Jüngsten Tag erweck mich, Herr,
> Dass ich dich schaue ewiglich.
> Amen, Amen, erhöre mich! [39]

During his last years in Leipzig Bach had noticeably become isolated. He had deliberately resisted the tendencies of his day; as time went on, his opposition to these movements had increased. His sons, pupils, and successors were attracted more to those of his works that had emanated from him in Weimar and Köthen than to those that he had written in Leipzig. The youngest of his sons referred to his father as an "old periwig."

Thus it was that the last three years of the master's life passed quietly within the narrow confines

---

[38] No. 522 in *The Lutheran Hymnal.*

[39] Before Thy throne I come and pray:
Cast not Thy sinful child away!
Do not Thy gracious help remove
From me who needs forgiving love!

A blessed end do Thou, Lord, give;
And then, that I with Thee may live,
Awaken me by Thy great power.
Amen. Oh, help me in this hour!

of a family circle as we might have expected to find it in the home of a German Lutheran cantor. Bach was content to be "a faithful father, who has the best interests of his children at heart," as he wrote to his cousin Elias Bach. At his side stood his spouse and performed her official duties as housewife and mother. Even though she was somewhat sickly, she found time to indulge her love for birds and flowers. She was "as delighted by a yellow carnation as is a little child by the holy Christ Child."

Even while the master was still suffering from a grievous malady of the eyes (cataracts), Count Brühl, the *Premierminister* of Saxony, had recommended his *Hauskapellmeister*, Joh. Gottlob Harrer, as the successor of Bach in Leipzig. Harrer had been educated in Italy and was said to be "thoroughly familiar with the brilliant style of music fashionable today."

With unseemly haste a trial performance was scheduled, and was held on June 8, 1749. Riemer's Chronicle of Leipzig states: "On June 8 . . . the trial performance for the future appointment as cantor of St. Thomas, in case the *Kapellmeister* and Cantor Mr. Sebastian Bach should die, was given in the large musical concert room . . . with greatest applause." [40] Bach, the out-of-date St. Thomas cantor, the "old periwig," was replaced by the up-to-date representative of the spirit of the day — the spirit prevailing in courtly circles and in Romance countries.

The eager candidate for Bach's office was the apostle of the new musical sentimentalism, an at-

[40] *The Bach Reader,* p. 185.

134

titude which demanded a "delicate and touching melody" in the style of Hasse and Graun. This was the way that Johann Christian, Bach's youngest son, was destined to travel. He became organist at the Catholic Cathedral in Milan. In London, he composed operas and symphonies in the fashion accepted by the "smart set" of the day. As a composer of clavier pieces, he exerted an influence on the youthful Mozart.

Without this intervention on the part of Brühl, the new St. Thomas cantor would probably have been Philipp Emanuel Bach or the prominent and faithful Bach disciple, Joh. Ludwig Krebs. Meanwhile, however, the area of church music, too, had been affected by far-reaching changes. Friedrich Doles, Bach's second successor in the cantorate of St. Thomas, rejected "those compositions of church music that contain only artificial fugues or that are fugal in character and whose development reveals nothing but scrupulous and meticulous concern for the strict rules and artificialities of double counterpoint." These, he insists, are only "achievements of the intellect; at best they can provide delight only for connoisseurs." Doles adds:

> Far be it from me to depreciate this higher form of composition or even to reject it. I myself have been a pupil of the now sainted Sebastian Bach and have written many compositions in the fugal manner. No! I merely disapprove of the inappropriate use that is sometimes made of this art. If my audience consists of learned musicians, I (would) gladly present a thoroughly developed fugue on the

135

organ, etc. But I would not use such material as church music in public worship of God or with the hope of moving uneducated listeners.

Bach's Necrology (obituary) informs us that the master's naturally somewhat weak eyesight, further weakened by his unheard-of zeal in studying, which made him, particularly in his youth, sit at work the whole night through, led, in his last years, to an eye disease. He wished to rid himself of this by an operation, partly out of a desire to be of further service to God and his neighbor with his other spiritual and bodily powers, which were still very vigorous, and partly on the advice of some of his friends, who placed great confidence in an oculist who had recently arrived in Leipzig. But the operation, although it had to be repeated, turned out very badly. Not only could he no longer use his eyes, but his whole system, which was otherwise thoroughly healthy, was completely overthrown by the operation and by the addition of harmful medicaments and other things, so that, thereafter, he was almost continuously ill for full half a year. Ten days before his death his eyes suddenly seemed better, so that one morning he could see quite well again and could also again endure the light. But a few hours later he suffered a stroke; and this was followed by a raging fever, as a victim of which, despite every possible care given him by two of the most skillful physicians of Leipzig, on the 28th day of July, 1750, a little after a quarter to nine in the evening, in the sixty-sixth year of his life, he quietly and peacefully, by the merit of his Redeemer, departed this life.[41]

[41] Ibid., p. 220.

Three days later the mortal remains of Sebastian Bach were buried on the Johannisfriedhof (cemetery).

Of Bach's twenty children only five sons and four daughters survived their father. His widow died in poverty as "Almosenfrau" (woman in need of alms). His youngest daughter also suffered acute need in old age. She received a little support, however, when Friedrich Rochlitz and Breitkopf & Härtel solicited financial help to relieve her condition, an appeal to which no less a person than Beethoven responded, sending the income he had obtained from his oratorio, *Christ on the Mount of Olives*.

The Necrology declares:

If ever a composer showed polyphony in its greatest strength, it was certainly our late lamented Bach. If ever a musician employed the most hidden secrets of harmony with the most skilled artistry, it was certainly our Bach. No one ever showed so many ingenious and unusual ideas as he in elaborate pieces such as ordinarily seem dry exercises in craftsmanship. He needed only to have heard any theme to be aware — it seemed in the same instant — of almost every intricacy that artistry could produce in the treatment of it. His melodies were strange, but always varied, rich in invention, and resembling those of no other composer. His serious temperament drew him by preference to music that was serious, elaborate, and profound; but he could also, when the occasion demanded, adjust himself, especially in playing, to a lighter and more humorous way of thought. His constant practice in the working out of polyphonic pieces had given his eye such facility that even in the largest scores he could take in all the simultaneously sounding parts at a glance. His hearing was so fine that he was able to detect the slightest error even in the largest ensembles. It is but a pity that it was only seldom he had the good fortune of finding a body of such performers as could have spared him unpleasant discoveries of this nature. In conducting he was very accurate, and of the tempo, which he generally took very lively, he was uncommonly sure.[42]

In his poem composed in memory of the Saint Thomas cantor, G. Philipp Telemann singles out characteristic traits of the departed master that had been decisive for his time and contemporaries. In the sonnet that Telemann wrote he celebrates Bach, the German, as the greatest master of instrumental music and as the superior master teacher of important pupils and sons. Of the latter group Telemann's godchild, Ph. Emanuel, of Berlin, the intended successor of his father in the St. Thomas cantorate, was the best known.

We see, then, that when Telemann exalts Bach he finds in him, not the creator of immortal masterworks, but the organ virtuoso and the master teacher:

Let Italy go on her virtuosi vaunting
Who through the sounding art have there achieved great
    fame —
On German soil they also will not be found wanting,
Nor can they here be held less worthy of the name.
Departed Bach! Long since thy splendid organ playing
Alone brought thee the noble cognomen "the Great,"
And what thy pen had writ, the highest art displaying,
Did some with joy and some with envy contemplate.
Then sleep! The candle of thy fame ne'er low will burn;

[42] Ibid., p. 222.

The pupils thou hast trained, and those they train in turn
Prepare thy future crown of glory brightly glowing.
Thy children's hands adorn it with its jewels bright,
But what shall cause thy true worth to be judged aright
Berlin to us now in a worthy son is showing.[43]

"Even if we carefully weigh everything that could
testify against him, this Leipzig Cantor remains a
manifestation of God: plain, yet not to be ex-
plained!"[44]

[43] Ibid., p. 227.

[44] Zelter in a letter to Goethe (1827).

BIBLIOGRAPHY

Besch, Hans. *Johann Sebastian Bach, Frömmigkeit und Glaube,* Vol. I. Kassel and Basel, 1938. Second edition, 1950.

Besseler, Heinrich. "J. S. Bach als Wegbereiter," *Archiv für Musikwissenschaft,* Jahrgang XII. Trossingen, 1955.

————. *J. S. Bach und das Mittelalter.* (A report from the "Bachtagung" of the Gesellschaft für Musikforschung, Leipzig, 1951)

Blume, Friedrich. J. S. Bach. (A reprint of the article on J. S. Bach in *Die Musik in Geschichte und Gegenwart,* Vol. I, Kassel and Basel, 1951. Detailed bibliography)

David, Hans and Arthur Mendel. *The Bach Reader.* New York, 1945.

Dufourcq, Norbert. *J. S. Bach, le maître de l'orgue.* Paris, 1948.

Forkel, Johann Nikolaus. *Über J. S. Bachs Leben, Kunst und Kunstwerke.* Leipzig, 1802. (A facsimile edition of this work, edited by J. M. Müller-Blattau, was published by the Bärenreiter Verlag, Kassel and Basel, 1950)

Geiringer, Karl. *The Bach Family.* New York, 1954. (Contains a detailed bibliography)

————. *Music of the Bach Family: An Anthology.* Cambridge, 1955.

Gurlitt, Wilibald. *J. S. Bach in seiner Zeit und Heute.* (A report from the "Bachtagung" of the Gesellschaft für Musikforschung, Leipzig, 1951)

141

————. *Die Musikerfamilie Bach* (Neue deutsche Biographie, Band I). München, 1953.

Hoelty-Nickel, Theodore, ed. *The Little Bach Book.* Valparaiso, 1950.

Pirro, Andre. *L'esthétique de J. S. Bach.* Paris, 1907.

Schering, Arnold. *Bach und das Musikleben Leipzigs im 18. Jahrhundert.* Leipzig, 1941.

Schmitz, Arnold. *Die Bildlichkeit der wortgebundenen Musik J. S. Bachs.* Mainz, 1950.

Schrade, Leo. *J. S. Bach, The Conflict Between the Sacred and the Secular.* New York, 1946.

Schweitzer, Albert. *J. S. Bach, le musicien poète.* Paris, 1905. Enlarged German edition. Leipzig, 1908. English translation from the German edition by Ernest Newman with alterations and additions by the author. London, 1911.

Spitta, Philipp. *J. S. Bach.* 2 vols. Leipzig, 1873, 1880. English translation by Clara Bell and J. A. Fuller Maitland. 3 vols. London, 1883—85. American edition, 2 vols. New York, 1951.

INDEX

144

145

London 135
Lorber, Johann Christoph 68
Luebeck, Vincent 36
Lueneburg, young Bach sings in the Michaeliskirche of 35
Luther's hymns 112; *see also* 129
works prominent in Bach's library 78
Lutheran liturgy, 106 f., 112, 115
Lutheranism, Bach's militant 79

Marchand, Louis 41, 62
Magnificat 105
Mass in B minor 105, 119 f.
Mattheson, 42, 88, 97
Moralism contrasted with Christianity 75; *see also* 112
Motet, Bach's use of 106; *see also* 107
Mozart 76, 135
Muehlhausen 79
Bach serves as organist in 43
Music, Bach clung to a Biblical foundation and aim for 44
courtly, contrasted with that of town musicians 62
joined with philosophy and theology 69
religious view of 31, 43 to 44, 70, 81, 96, 100, 112, 123, 130
Musical education 102
Musical Offering 127, 132

"Musician, the fortunate" 67, 70, 94
Mysticism 10, 76—77
scantily represented in Bach's library 78

Neo-romanticism in music 93
Neumeister, Erdmann 74—75, 96, 109
Nietzsche, Friedrich 102, 118
"Notenbuch" of Anna Magdalena Bach 95
Numbers, composers' use of 67—68, 72—73

Ohrdruf
The orphaned Bach lived with his brother in 33 to 35
Bach attended the "Gymnasium" in 35, 78
Old-fashioned, Bach's contemporaries considered him 90, 112, 131, 133—134
Opera 63, 75
Bach extremely careful in adapting devices of 50
Orchestra, Bach's 92—93, 104
Organ
Bach's virtuosity on and knowledge of 56; *see also* 37
central in Bach's art 37 f.
design, Bach's idea of 58—59
tone, Bach's idea of 58
works, Bach's Weimar period 55, 65
Orgelbüchlein 67, 82, 123
Orthodox theologians fostered music 43—44